Real Money Questions

Real Money Questions 101

The African American Financial Question and Answer Book

JESSE B. BROWN

An Amber Book

John Wiley & Sons, Inc.

Published by John Wiley & Sons, Inc., Hoboken, New Jersey
Published simultaneously in Canada

Produced by Amber Books Publishing, 1334 East Chandler Boulevard, Suite 5-D67, Phoenix, AZ 85048, Tony Rose, Publisher and Editorial Director; Samuel P. Peabody, Associate Publisher; Yvonne Rose, Senior Editor

Design and production by Navta Associates, Inc.

For general information about our other products and services, please contact our Customer Care Department within the United States at (800) 762-2974, outside the United States at (317) 572-3993 or fax (317) 572-4002.

Wiley also publishes its books in a variety of electronic formats. Some content that appears in print may not be available in electronic books. For more information about Wiley products, visit our web site at www.wiley.com.

Library of Congress Cataloging-in-Publication Data:

Brown, Jesse B.
    101 real money questions : the African American financial question and answer book / Jesse B. Brown.
        p. cm.
"An Amber book."
Includes index.
    ISBN 0-471-20674-1 (pbk.)
    1. African Americans—Finance, Personal—Examinations, questions, etc. 2. Finance, Personal—Examinations, questions, etc. 3. Investments—Examinations, questions, etc.
I. Title: One hundred one real money questions. II Title.
    HG179 .B74645 2003
    332.024'0396073—dc21   2002014418

Printed in the United States of America

To my wife, Delores, who inspires,
and my daughter, Khalilah,
who validates all that I do

Acknowledgments

I'd like to thank especially Carole Hall, editor in chief, African American Books, John Wiley & Sons, Inc.; Tony Rose, publisher and CEO, Amber Books Publishing; Yvonne Rose, senior editor, Amber Books Publishing; Lynette McMillon, the Tushe Group, my publicist, for her diligence and dedication to this project; Jan Miller, my literary agent; Tavis Smiley of the Tavis Smiley Foundation; and Denise Pines of the Tavis Smiley Foundation.

I have not attempted to cite in the text all the authorities and sources consulted in the preparation of this book. The list would include departments of the federal government, libraries, industrial institutions, periodicals, and many individuals. Scores of people have contributed information, illustrations, and inspirations toward the publishing of *101 Real Money Questions: The African American Financial Question and Answer Book*.

Contents

About the Author

Jesse B. Brown is a graduate of the Kellogg School of Management at Northwestern University, Evanston, Illinois, where he was named Alumnus of the Year. He is the past president of the National Association of Securities Professionals—Chicago Chapter and has earned Investment Adviser of the Year honors from one of the largest mutual fund companies in America.

Before joining the financial services industry, Brown served as Special Assistant to the President of the Joint Center for Political Studies in Washington, D.C., and as Deputy to the Assistant Secretary of the Treasury under President Jimmy Carter. He later joined Kidder Peabody as a stockbroker specializing in municipal markets.

Jesse B. Brown is known as one of the country's most renowned financial planners. He is president/CEO and Midwest managing director of Krystal Investment Management, Inc., which oversees millions of dollars in mutual funds, stocks, and bonds for its investor clients. According to Brown: "As African Americans, we must realize the significance of paying ourselves first and investing in ourselves, our families, our children, our schools, our churches, our businesses, and our communities. We must see ourselves realistically in our society and project what we want to be and put the plan in order. Then, we, as a burgeoning and vibrant independent people, will begin to see most of our goals and commitments realized."

Jesse B. Brown has written *101 Real Money Questions: The African American Financial Question and Answer Book* as the third step in your journey toward financial independence. His first book, *Investing in the Dream,* was a bestseller on *Essence* magazine's Black Board Best Seller's List for hardcover nonfiction books and was selected as the 2001 Chicago Black Book Fair's Book of the Year. His second book, *Pay Yourself First: The African American Guide to Financial Success and Security,* was a top 10 nonfiction *Essence* magazine pick, a national bestseller, and again selected as the 2002 Chicago Black Book Fair's Book of the Year.

Foreword

For years I have been preaching to Black folk the importance of getting up and making a difference. One very significant way to make a difference is to have some money in your pocket. When you have money in your pocket, many of life's challenges become manageable: medical insurance to cover emergency health examinations, surgeries, expensive treatments, and prescriptions becomes affordable; college tuition for your son or daughter, who despite the obstacles has worked hard to get good grades in high school, becomes fundable; retirement for you and your spouse, without the worry of income to pay the bills, becomes a realistic goal; care for your aging parents, in your home if you choose, is not a concern. Money in your pocket is one of the best defenses against anxiety and frustration, and if used positively, can most assuredly add to your sense of freedom.

When it comes to money matters, Black folk have over six hundred million dollars in disposable income, enough to be the eleventh-largest nation in the world, but almost nothing in the way of investments. We think we have all the time in the world to plan for our financial futures. We tell ourselves that we'll take care of it tomorrow, but tomorrow becomes the next day and the next day and the next. Procrastination is the most convenient response to the challenge of paying attention to your financial affairs. Many have already determined that finance is far too difficult to understand and far too daunting to undertake. What is the stock market, anyway? What do you mean by mutual funds? How does retirement roll over? It all can sound much more difficult than it really is. Most of us would love to not get down on the field and be a player, but to stay on the sidelines and watch the game of life proceed without direct involvement, believing that things will work themselves out. It has been said that the best way to predict your future is to create it. Things don't just happen; you claim your destiny! And that is what *101 Real Money Questions: The African American Financial Question and Answer Book* is all about. With *101 Real Money Questions,* the information is put out there for you to read, absorb, and act on. Jesse Brown puts money in your pocket, answers all your questions, and gives you the know-how to create the future you want for yourself and your family.

For fiscally challenged individuals, Jesse Brown inspires hope. Managing your financial affairs is possible. Paying for the services, needs, and desires of you and your family is possible. Creating wealth for you and your family can be as real as the breath you breathe. I have tremendous admiration for Jesse because he takes our human rights movement to the next level. We have all sorts of freedoms these days, thanks to our ancestors, family members, and other loved ones who refused to accept less. Now it's up to us to refuse to accept mediocrity, and pick up where they left off. It's up to us to win the one freedom that remains elusive—financial freedom, financial stability. Jesse assures us that mastering the skills needed to manage money isn't difficult. We would be remiss in our responsibility to ourselves and our families if we did not gain the upper hand over our money. Such an outcome can be more than merely expensive—it can be devastating to our lives and those of our children.

Jesse puts into print the same message he delivers to his clients: "Educate yourself, get a plan, and take charge of your financial life." To that I would add, find yourself a knowledgeable financial adviser—one who can help you create your individual financial plan, select the appropriate investments, and stay on track, but who, in the final analysis, leaves you in full control. This book's important message is to hold the vision of the possibility of a better life for you and yours and to make that vision a reality by securing your financial future. Take responsibility and exercise the faith and power you have within you to create a better life by investing.

In this compact volume of questions and answers, Jesse covers the principles of building wealth and discusses mutual funds, an ideal investment vehicle for achieving that end. He talks about one of the biggest mistakes many people make with their money—debt—and counsels on how to avoid missteps, or at least how to dampen their potentially negative effects. He discusses how best to use insurance to provide financial security for loved ones and to protect possessions. Through use of his advanced educational degrees and significant national leadership positions and extensive financial services experiences, Jesse brings Wall Street to the hood, so to speak, with what could be an otherwise daunting subject—personal finance. It is easy to become a victim, and oftentimes that is perceived as a comfortable position to be in. Each one of us has individual needs and wants, and our separate story to tell. In *101 Real Money Questions,* Jesse Brown answers our questions about money and shows us how to take as little as 5 dollars a day and turn it into a million dollars through saving and investing.

Above all, Jesse urges immediate action, for time can be a powerful ally—or without a sound financial plan, a devastating enemy.

Tavis Smiley
The Smiley Group, Inc.

Introduction

You can't get away from it. From television to the Internet to barbershops, everyone's talking about money. They always have, but now it seems different. Everywhere you look, someone's touting a stock tip that earned him millions, a newscaster is professing the end of Social Security, or you hear tales of a millionaire gone bankrupt. People who've never invested before are dabbling in stocks. The company you've been with for twenty years is folding. College tuition is rising. Real estate is rising. The little country home you dreamed about retiring in has tripled in cost. Your daughter had a medical emergency and you just used your retirement savings to pay for it.

Someone told you to invest in an IRA, but you don't know what that is. Someone else said you could save money in a tax-deferred account, but you don't know where to find one. Then there's the pressure of looking rich. Every movie and music video you see is another reminder of what you don't have. You just purchased a gold Lexus, not sure how you'll make the payments and live happily. The pressure is bearing in. Your savings are diminished and your checking account never builds. Stocks and bonds are foreign to you.

What do you do? Where do you start?

A sampling of comments from listeners of my audiotape series and my appearances on radio programs across the country, as well as from readers of my articles, newsletters, and books, indicates you can start where you are.

Marc R. stated that I helped him because he is "hungry for success in the market." Benitez M., after reading my book *Investing in the Dream,* is now properly motivated and educated to exceed his current level of investments.

Karen H., a wife and mother of two, stated after reading my second book, *Pay Yourself First: The African American Guide to Financial Success and Security,* that it was the first financial book that was easy to read and made sense, and which spoke directly to her needs and convinced her that she could retire comfortably.

My third book in the "Pay Yourself First" series, *101 Real Money Questions: The African American Financial Question and Answer Book,* is your opportunity to get your questions answered.

I am a "Financial Makeover" columnist for abcnews.com and the financial expert at Tavis Smiley's Web site, tavistalks.com, as well as a columnist for more than 240 Black newspapers through the Black Press of America, National Newspaper Publishers Association (NNPA). I am also president and CEO of Krystal Investment Management, a national money management firm. I get questions all the time about personal finances investing, and in this book I'll answer those questions.

It's time to get our finances in order. Too many African American families are living paycheck to paycheck, with minimal retirement savings and too much frivolous spending. To achieve any sense of financial stability in your life, you must stop, assess what you have, budget, save, and invest.

It's reeducation time. African Americans spend over $400 billion annually. But how much do we save? African Americans who earn more than $50,000 annually save less than their European American counterparts, yet they profess to want to retire early. You see, even those who have higher incomes haven't achieved success if their savings and investments are minimal. So where are we?

We are on the final frontier of the civil rights movement: financial freedom. Urgings to invest and save are slowly pouring from civil rights havens and Black churches and colleges alike. Why? Because the time is now! African Americans are among the world's highest spenders, but we have minimal savings. Why? Because too many of us don't understand wealth, how it is amassed, or how to keep it. Most of America's millionaires are not entertainers or athletes, as the media would lead us to believe. Most are hardworking citizens with a knack for long-term saving and investing. Stock investments, portfolios, and financial plans are what separate the haves from the have-nots.

In this day and age, there is no excuse for lackadaisical financial planning. There is just too much information at our fingertips. But you must harness this information and stick with it. It's not easy, but it is worth it. Do you want to go through another decade without accumulating wealth, real wealth that will ensure a comfortable retirement, pay for education for your children, and give you a freedom never before experienced? Or do you want to continue to scrape, always a dollar short and a day late, purchasing things you don't need to feel better about your shattered finances?

The choice is yours. Financial remedies are as simple as reading a book on finances, reading financial articles—and better yet, reading this book.

This book is designed to teach African Americans how to amass the wealth they desire through saving and investing. There are no magic potions, no get-rich-quick schemes. Just time-honored methods that will guarantee financial success.

All that is required of those who desire is discipline. You must set up a plan and stick with it. In the end, your financial success depends on you.

Jesse B. Brown
Krystal Investment Management

Chapter 1

Setting Financial Goals

TIP Develop strategies that, once in place, will help you to roll with short-term swings, confident that your overall long-term goals will be met.

Things such as losing weight or quitting smoking may top your list of resolutions, but getting your financial life in order is just as important. I have already shown thousands and thousands of African Americans how to successfully manage their money and make even more while they're doing it. When new clients ask me what their resolutions should be, I say:

- Review your investment portfolio once a year. It is important to make sure you're on track to meeting your goals.
- Fund a retirement plan. If you are currently contributing to a 401(k) or other employer-sponsored plan, see if there is any way to increase your contribution. If you do not contribute to a plan, set one up and commit to saving a certain amount each month.
- Review your insurance coverage. Analyze your home, auto, life, disability, and health policies to make sure you have adequate coverage and fair premiums.

- Create or update a will. If you don't have an up-to-date will, see your attorney. A will is essential for making sure your assets will be distributed according to your wishes.
- Prepare a budget. Look at your monthly expenses and account for irregular expenses such as Christmas gifts or unexpected home repairs. Consider using one of the many computer software programs available to make this a quick and easy task.
- Eliminate credit card debt. Make it a goal to pay off any balances you have on credit cards. Credit card debt carries high interest rates, and paying off your balance will free up money that you can save or invest.

Anyone can learn the financial rules of the road. The trick is to start. That's the hardest part.

Five Easy Steps

If you are ready for financial freedom, let this book be your guide. If you are ready to take these five easy steps, we can get going:

1. Review your current financial situation. You need to have a realistic understanding of where you stand as far as assets, liabilities, savings, and so on. Once you know your current situation, you can plan for the future.
2. Set goals. Think about what you want and need to do in the future. Financial goals can be very diverse—anything from traveling six months out of the year to paying for grandchildren to go to college. Also think about when you will need this money.
3. Develop a plan of action. Once you know how much you need, you should develop a plan to help you get there. Selecting investments that fit your goals and risk tolerance is essential to forming a plan you will stick with over the long term.
4. Be consistent. Whether it's a dollar cost averaging investment program or weekly savings goals, you must do what you committed to in your financial plan.

5. Review your progress. Once you've started implementing your plan, you will want to see how you are progressing. Look at your quarterly statements and make sure you understand what's going on. If you want your plan to help you meet your goals, you need to review it regularly.

The Problem with Procrastinating

Procrastinating is harmful in every aspect of our lives, but especially when it comes to our finances. Saying you'll save more money after you get that job or you buy that new house or the kids are done with school is a dangerous habit to get into.

It's helpful to look ahead and realize that if you don't start saving now, your retirement won't be all you hoped it would be. When you save money early, the power of compounding can potentially benefit you for your diligence over time.

TIP Developing a habit now of saving and planning for the long term is very important.

Parents Lead the Way

My daughters seem to live hand-to-mouth. They do not have savings accounts for their children, they stopped paying into the investment plans that I started for their children, they have no wills, and they constantly let their life insurance policies lapse. I know times are hard for all of us, but I have always believed that if you have kids you should make plans in the event you can no longer care for them. How can I convince my daughters to take better care of their children's financial future?

Erma M. of St. Louis, MO

Erma, you sound like a very responsible mother and grandmother. There are several important benefits that will help convince your daughters to follow a more responsible financial road for your grandchildren. The more you know about your money, the more able you will be to:

- Talk to your children about money. Show your children and grandchildren, by example, how to save and manage money. This can help equip them for a lifetime of responsible financial decisions.
- Help your children put money away now for college for your grandchildren. Even if you can only start out with small amounts, they need to start saving now for college costs.
- Purchase sufficient insurance. Make sure you have enough life insurance to provide for your children and grandchildren. Also ensure that you have adequate disability insurance.
- Save for your retirement. It's important. Your retirement money may help your grandchildren through college one day.
- Gift assets to your children. If you plan to leave your assets to your children, you may want to make annual gifts during your lifetime. This not only reduces the value of your estate for tax purposes but also allows you to watch how your children use their gifts and share in their joy.

Financial Planning for African American Women

I am a fifty-year-old woman with a great career and three grown children. I am engaged to a sixty-year-old man with no children and lots of money. I am in love, and have no desire to bury my husband-to-be, but I know statistics say that I probably will out-live him. Give me some tips on how to develop a financial plan that will help me in the event he dies before I do.

Joyce S. of Mount Vernon, NY

Whether they are executives, entrepreneurs, mothers, or teachers, many women hold substantial wealth and are in need of solid financial planning advice. Since the roles women play vary so much, each woman has unique needs. However, there are several common areas of concern.

Investment planning is one important issue for most women. Selecting investments that are appropriate for your financial goals and situation is key to creating a plan that will help meet your needs.

Consider your investment objectives and make sure your plan takes into account your:

- Financial resources
- Time horizon
- Future needs
- Risk tolerance

It may be wise to entrust this planning to a financial professional. That way, once your plan is formulated, you just need to follow it and leave the periodic monitoring to your financial planner.

Another area of importance to women is estate planning. It doesn't matter if a woman has inherited her husband's estate or acquired her own through work or investments—all women should review the estate planning options available. Things such as making lifetime gifts to reduce estate tax burdens, using trusts for minor children or grandchildren, and making charitable contributions are all possibilities women should understand to decide what is best for their situation.

Planning for retirement is also a key concern for women. Whether they have their own retirement plan through an employer or inherit their spouse's retirement plan, they will need to make decisions about those retirement benefits. Questions such as "What distribution option is best for me?" and "Will my retirement nest egg be enough to live on?" must be answered, and women need to be able to make knowledgeable decisions.

TIP Establishing a financial plan is an essential part in helping to ensure that we meet our financial goals. It's not a difficult process, but it does require some time and effort.

A variety of concerns exist for women to consider in planning their financial lives. Since no two women are exactly alike, there is not an easy answer to any of these questions. Seeking the advice of a trusted financial professional is one way that women can wade through these issues and work to achieve their financial goals.

Three Steps toward Meeting Your Financial Goals

1. The first step in establishing a financial plan is assessing your current financial situation.

2. The next step is identifying your financial goals. You need to think in specific terms in order to establish goals you can work to achieve. Maybe you want to travel after retirement, move to a different state, or stay at home and enjoy your hobbies.

3. Once you have identified your priorities for the future, the third step is deciding how to reach those goals by sifting through the many investment vehicles to determine which products are most appropriate for your situation.

Start to Build Wealth at Any Age

I am a recent high school graduate. I can't play basketball or rap, hate jail, and love life. Since I got good grades in school, I was able to get a scholarship to Tennessee State University. My plans after college include earning lots of money and getting my mom out of the projects. Where do I start?

Anton W. of Detroit, MI

Wealth building requires organization, planning, and motivation. To help in that quest, remember the following principles:

- The first step to building wealth is making the decision to do so. Set a goal and then begin mapping out a strategy to achieve it.

- Money begets money. When you save and invest a portion of your income, you can begin to reap the benefits of money that is working for you.
- Spend less than you earn. Save at least 5 percent of everything you make; 10 percent is even better.
- Earn interest, don't pay it. Put your credit cards away, except for emergencies, and reduce your installment debt to zero. This will help you begin to pay yourself rather than your creditors.
- Put time on your side. If you have ambitious financial goals, one of the best moves you can make is to start saving as soon as possible.
- Be consistent. Many savings plans fail because people don't have the motivation to consistently invest over the long term. Your goal should be to build wealth gradually, steadily, and consistently.
- Pay yourself first. If you pay all your bills each month and then try to save what's left, you'll probably find little left. Instead, treat your wealth-accumulation plan as a bill—money you owe yourself.
- Protect your assets. Make sure you have adequate medical, homeowners, life, and disability insurance. This protects you and your family from the unexpected.

Five Tips to Start With

I just got engaged to a man who has promised me the moon and stars. It appears that he may be able to deliver. Before the wedding day, I need some tips on how to increase my net worth.

Frances H. of Baltimore, MD

To achieve your financial goals, you need to find ways to increase your net worth, which can be accomplished by increasing your assets and/or decreasing your debts. These five basic tips can help:

1. Set rewarding financial goals. Putting money aside for a distant goal, rather than spending that money now, is a difficult thing

for most people to do. So set goals that will reward you and motivate you to achieve them. Then quantify your ultimate goal as well as interim goals, so you'll have a way to track your progress.

2. Spend less than you earn. The amount of money left over for saving is a direct result of your lifestyle. Your lifestyle decisions will affect you now and in the future, since you will probably want to continue the same lifestyle after retirement. To get a grip on your spending, take time to analyze your expenses and to set a budget. Try reducing nonessential expenditures. Another strategy is to find ways to spend less money for the same things.

3. Save it before you see it. If you have to find the money for saving every month, you'll likely find that there isn't much left after all the bills are paid. Typically, a better strategy is to set up an automatic savings program in which money is automatically deducted from your bank account every month and deposited directly in an investment account. Another good alternative is to sign up for your company's 401(k) plan, having funds withdrawn every paycheck. (Remember that an automatic investing plan, such as dollar cost averaging, does not assure a profit or protect against a loss in declining markets. Since such a strategy involves periodic investment, consider your financial ability and willingness to continue purchases through periods of low price levels.)

4. Don't let debt sabotage your goals. If a significant portion of your income is going to pay interest on your loans, that leaves less available for saving. Strive to eliminate all your debts except your mortgage.

5. Invest, don't just save. Your ultimate nest egg will be a function of two factors—how much you save and how much you earn on those savings.

TIP Become familiar with various investment alternatives so that you'll feel comfortable investing in more aggressive alternatives that offer potentially higher rates of return.

Make Sure to Follow Through

Preparing a comprehensive financial plan can be a difficult and complicated task. To help assure that your plan helps you accomplish your goals, consider the following tips:

- Take action on your plan. You need to make sure to implement the actions outlined in the plan, which requires commitment and dedication on your part.

- Review your plan at least annually. Changes in your personal situation may necessitate changes to your goals and implementation strategy. Those can include events outside your control, such as a major stock market decline, or personal circumstances, such as getting married, having a baby, losing your job, getting divorced, and retiring.

- Maintain a long-term perspective. Many financial goals take years to accomplish. For instance, you may need to start saving for retirement twenty or thirty years before you actually retire. Maintaining the commitment to accomplish that goal over such a long time can be difficult.

- Consider using a professional who can provide assistance in areas you are unfamiliar with, such as estate planning or investment strategies, and can also help monitor your progress. Sometimes it's easier to stay committed to long-term goals if you know someone else is also watching your progress.

Working on Your Financial Goals

My former boyfriend was a great financial analyst. He mapped out everything for me and kept me on track. That was the only part of our relationship that worked, because he has some of the most irritating habits of anyone I know. I had to dump him to maintain my sanity. But now that he is gone, I don't know how to keep on track of my financial goals.

Eva T. of Powder Springs, GA

What steps are you taking to help ensure that you are making progress toward your financial goals? Developing and following a written financial plan will give you a road map to help you accomplish them. The six steps involved in that process are:

1. Assess your current financial situation.

This involves preparing a net worth statement. List your assets and liabilities—the difference represents your net worth. Periodically preparing a net worth statement will help you assess whether you are making progress toward your goals.

You should also analyze how you spend your income. Prepare a cash flow statement, detailing your income and expenditures by category for the past year. Even if you haven't been keeping track of expenditures, looking at canceled checks, credit card receipts, and tax returns will provide much of the needed information. If you can't account for large sums, keep a journal of all expenditures for a month. You are likely to be surprised by the amount spent on nonessential items like dining out, entertainment, clothing, and vacations. This awareness may be enough to cause you to reduce your spending. If not, prepare a budget for future spending that incorporates your financial goals.

2. Establish written, specific financial goals.

Your goals should be defined in specific, quantifiable terms, so you have a means to measure your progress. Be sure to attach a timetable to each goal. If you have several financial goals, you should prioritize them so you devote resources to those most important to you. The most common long-term goals include:

- Financial independence (at retirement or sooner)
- College education for children
- Debt reduction
- A desired lifestyle
- Business ownership
- Major charitable giving

3. *Develop a detailed plan, with specific strategies and time-tables.*

Your financial plan should coordinate strategies in several important areas:

- *Investment strategies.* Determine what investments should be used for your savings. Develop a strategy you are comfortable with, taking into account a reasonable risk level and your time frame for investing.
- *Tax planning strategies.* Reducing your income taxes can provide additional funds for saving.
- *Debt strategies.* While debt may be necessary to help achieve some goals, such as home ownership, you should develop ways to avoid incurring excessive amounts of debt.
- *Risk management strategies.* To ensure your plan won't be derailed by catastrophes, assess your life, health, disability income, property, and liability insurance. Also make sure you have an emergency fund covering several months' living expenses.
- *Estate planning strategies.* Proper estate planning helps ensure that your wealth is distributed according to your wishes at a minimal estate tax cost.

4. *Implement your financial plan.*

Carrying out your plan requires a lifetime of discipline and dedication. Make saving and investing part of your monthly routine so they become strong habits. Don't become overwhelmed by the amounts you need to save, since it often takes years to see substantial progress toward your goals. Don't try to accomplish too much, or you may become disillusioned with your entire plan. Strive to make slow and steady progress.

5. *Monitor your progress.*

At least annually, review your progress toward your goals:

- Update your net worth statement and analysis of spending.
- Evaluate your investment performance.

Your Spouse and the Family Finances

In many families, one spouse takes primary responsibility for the family's finances, doing everything from paying bills to making investment decisions to reviewing insurance policies. If that spouse dies first, the other spouse may have difficulty taking over these tasks. Therefore, if you take care of money matters in your marriage, one of your more important financial duties is to prepare your spouse for handling the family's finances. Some strategies to consider include:

- Maintain good records. Financial records should be well organized, located in one central spot, and contain only pertinent information. Old or outdated information may confuse your spouse.

- Prepare written instructions. These instructions should cover everything from insurance policies to investments to company benefits to monthly bills, ensuring that nothing will be overlooked. Also list all your assets, why you own them, and where important documents are kept. Update these instructions at least annually.

- Discuss your finances with your spouse. Go over your written instructions, explaining your rationale for major financial decisions. Your death would likely necessitate changes in investment allocations, insurance policies, and other financial matters, so encourage your spouse to explore all options before making decisions.

- Involve your spouse in the family's finances now. Your spouse can start by paying monthly bills, balancing the checkbook, or reviewing credit card charges. Increase his or her involvement as confidence builds.

- Line up professionals for your spouse. Even if your spouse assumes some financial duties, there may be areas that he or she will never feel comfortable handling. Identify those areas, find knowledgeable professionals who can help, and introduce your spouse to those professionals now.

- Rebalance your investments if changes are needed to maintain your desired asset mix.
- Decide if any changes should be made to your financial goals.

6. Seek help with your plan.

While you can prepare a financial plan by yourself, there are some advantages to having a professional's help:

Developing a written financial plan is a complex process requiring coordination of all your finances. But the process is well worth the effort, since it gives you a road map to help achieve your financial goals. ■

- To obtain the advice of an objective person, knowledgeable in all areas of financial planning, who can ensure that significant concerns are not overlooked.
- To keep up-to-date on new developments in the financial arena.
- To ensure that all financial decisions make sense in the context of your overall financial plan.
- To help provide the discipline needed to implement your plan. You may be more inclined to follow your plan if you know someone else is also monitoring your progress.

Chapter 2

Starting Out—or Starting Over

Teaching Kids about Money

I am a grandmother of three. During the time that I raised my three children, money was tight, so I did not think that I could afford to save or invest money. This means that I could not teach my children the value of saving or investing money for the future. I want more for my grandchildren. What can I do to help my grandchildren understand that they do not need to spend every dime they get on video games and sneakers? The youngest grandchild is six; is that too soon to start?

Deborah B. of South Bend, IN

In previous generations, attitudes about money were different. Many of our parents and grandparents stashed money in banks and maybe had a pension plan, but there wasn't much education about investing. Today, however, it's a different story. We have available to us multitudes of options including the stock market, retirement plans, and individual retirement accounts (IRAs).

You can start teaching your grandchildren about money as early as age six.

> **TIP** We need to start teaching our children about investing at an early age so they will grow up to be responsible, financially secure adults.

19

Instead of giving them a weekly allowance, try assigning them different jobs around the house to earn money. When they receive their "wages," you can use that chance to explain the value of putting away money regularly. Show them how to deposit money in the bank and explain how their money will earn interest. As they start to understand this concept, consider giving them an incentive to save, such as contributing 50 cents for each dollar they save.

When your grandchildren are old enough, you can explain how a business operates and why people buy and sell stocks. You could have your child pick a stock he or she would like to purchase and then buy shares in a custodial account. That way they can learn about how the stock market works and about investing for the long term. Children will take a greater interest when it is their money that is invested, making this a great learning opportunity.

When children are young, you have the chance to teach them things they will hold to throughout their lives. Teaching children to understand the basics of investing and importance of saving is something that could pay dividends to you and them for the rest of your lives.

Finances and Your Marriage

I am the father of four grown children, and I am considering marriage for the second time. My first wife spent a lot of money on clothes and vacations. My fiancée has never been married and has a young child who she wants to send to college. My youngest child just graduated from college, and it has taken me a long time to recover financially from my marriage. Even though I love my fiancée and her son, I don't want a repeat of my first marriage. I need some pointers on how to discuss finances with my soon-to-be bride.

Harold R. of Oak Park, IL

Was it Moms Mabley, the noted African American comedian, who said, "Long after the sex is gone it's money that keeps the honey"? Money often plays a powerful role in determining the level of bliss or discord in a marriage. Fundamental disagreements over how to manage money could turn a relationship into a battle. If a couple has trouble seeing eye to eye on money issues, lacks common money goals, and can't agree on how to spend or how to save, their marriage may suffer. Money matters are typically a part of almost every decision a couple makes. Should we buy beef or chicken? Watch television or go out to a show? See Europe next summer or stay home and work on the house?

Working together to manage your financial affairs could help to improve your overall financial situation.

Dreams of a Better Future

My mother just passed and left me a life insurance policy settlement. Although it is not a great deal of money, it is enough to help my husband and me achieve some of our dreams. My husband wants to pay bills, but I say we will always have bills, so

---

Some tips to help prevent conflict regarding money in your marriage include:

- Remembering that marriage is an economic relationship . . . a personal business partnership. Actively manage your family's financial affairs; don't leave them to chance. Work together.

- Analyzing your attitudes toward money. Does one of you like to spend unexpected income, the other to save it? Does one feel comfortable with a full debt load, the other nervous about borrowing? Exchange points of view. Seek common ground through compromise.

- Sharing all money decisions and responsibilities. If nothing else, sit down together each week to pay bills.

---

why not find out about savings and investments. We are not sure where to start.

Audrey J. of Denver, CO

We all have dreams of a better future. We wish for a college education for our children, to travel and live where we desire, and to enjoy a leisurely, financially secure retirement. But wishes alone will not allow us to achieve our financial goals. The way to help you achieve these goals is to develop a realistic plan—and follow that plan to its conclusion.

Both short- and long-term goals need to be established. Short-term goals might include taking an exotic vacation, saving for a down payment on a house, or purchasing a new car. Long-term goals might include funding a child's college education or saving for retirement.

It is important to list your goals in specific and quantifiable terms. A goal of "helping pay for my child's college education" won't give you the means to determine when you have actually achieved the goal. A more appropriate goal would be "I want to pay for the entire cost of sending my eight-year-old child to a public university for four years."

List your goals in order of importance. Since we all have limited resources, you should start saving for the goals that are most important to you.

Once you have determined your goals, you should assess your current financial situation and develop a plan to help you achieve your goals. Learning to invest over a long period of time takes patience, discipline, and dedication. In many cases, progress may not be seen in a month or two, or even in a year or two.

Changing Financial Concerns

Hurray! Our youngest daughter just got married and moved out. My husband and I are now happy empty-nesters who are antici-pating his retirement from work soon. Some of our friends' chil-

dren along with their children have moved back home, so we have decided to avoid this by selling our home and traveling. How can we start to plan for our life without work- or child-related constraints?

Thelma L. of Atlanta, GA

At different points in your life, you will be concerned with different financial matters. While it is true that different individuals can face these phases earlier or later than other individuals, the cycle of issues proceeds in a fairly predictable pattern over your lifetime.

Your Twenties and Thirties

- Establish solid financial habits, since the money habits you develop now will set the financial tone for the rest of your life. Set up a record-keeping system, monitor your cash flow, and develop a workable budget.
- Start a regular savings program, aiming to save at least 10 percent of your gross income. Build a contingency fund.
- Invest for the long term.
- Most individuals are eager at this age to purchase their first home. First, make sure you can afford the mortgage payments without straining your budget.
- Start saving now for your children's college education.
- Prepare a will or trust. Make sure you name guardians for your minor children.

Your Forties and Fifties

- Your children are probably now in college and may need your help to finance their college education.
- At the same time, your parents may also need your help with financial matters.
- Make sure you start seriously saving for your retirement at this age. Evaluate your investments.
- Review your estate plan.

Your Sixties and Beyond

- Before retiring, review your finances carefully to ensure a financially secure retirement.
- Review your estate plan. Consider the use of a living will, a health-care proxy, a durable power of attorney, and a living trust.
- Reevaluate your gift-giving plans for your family and charities.

Achieving Debt-Free Status

When I graduated from college, I decided to start off with a bang. So I got a new job and bought a house and a car. Six years later I am in so much debt trying to keep up the house and other assorted bills. I want to wipe out my debt before it rubs me out. How?

Reggie M. of Gulfport, MS

Increasing debt levels can make it difficult to achieve your financial goals. If a significant portion of your income is going to pay interest on your loans, that leaves less available for saving and investing for your financial goals. While it may be difficult to achieve debt-free status when you own a home, it is a reasonable goal to owe no debts other than your mortgage. To help you with that goal, consider the following three steps:

1. Stop incurring new debt.

If you are truly committed to reducing debts, you must stop incurring additional debt. Only use your credit cards if you can pay the balance off in full every month. Instead, consider using a debit card, which automatically deducts charges from your checking account. If you don't have cash for a purchase, wait until you can save the money.

2. Consider consolidating debts with a lower-interest-rate option.

You may be able to transfer credit card and other debt balances to lower interest rate alternatives. However, don't implement this strategy until you have step one under control. You don't want to obtain a lower-interest-rate card and then just start adding new balances to it.

You may also want to consider a home-equity loan to pay off your consumer debt. Home-equity loans typically carry lower interest rates than other forms of personal loans, and as long as the balance does not exceed $100,000, interest paid on a home-equity loan is deductible on your tax return.

3. Prioritize and pay down your debts.

List all your debts—from the highest to the lowest interest rates—and your minimum monthly payments. Add up your minimum payments and then determine how much more you can add to pay down those debts. Rather than paying a little bit extra on each of your debts, use these additional funds to pay off the debt with the highest interest rate. Once that debt is paid in full, start paying the debt with the next highest interest rate, continuing until all your debt is paid in full.

Refinancing Your Home Mortgage

I bought my house one year ago, but since then the mortgage rates have dropped so that I want to refinance to a lower rate. Should I?

Linda Sue B. of Chicago Heights, IL

Recent interest rate cuts by the Federal Reserve have resulted in declining mortgage rates. The average rate on a thirty-year fixed-rate mortgage fell to a record low of 5.87 percent in September 2002 (Source: Reuters News Service). With such significant declines, you should review whether it makes financial sense to refinance now, even if you obtained your mortgage or refinanced a short time ago.

Refinancings historically were recommended when current mortgage rates were at least two percentage points lower than your existing mortgage rate. But that guideline assumed that the homeowner would pay significant refinancing costs, such as points, title insurance, appraisal fees, and other fees. Now many lenders offer refinancings with much lower costs. Thus, even if current mortgage rates are only half a percent lower than your current rate, investigate whether you should refinance.

As you go through the process, consider these tips:

■ Shop around among lenders, comparing all costs, including up-front expenses like credit checks and appraisals, total interest costs for at least five years, and closing costs. Some lenders may offer lower interest rates with higher up-front and closing costs. You need to evaluate the entire cost of the refinancing.

■ Determine whether it makes economic sense to refinance. Ask lenders to calculate the monthly mortgage payment and an estimate of all costs. Divide these costs by the after-tax savings in your monthly mortgage payment to see how long it will take to recover those costs. If you will recover the costs before you plan to move, you may want to refinance.

■ Consider switching your adjustable-rate mortgage (ARM) to a fixed rate. With lower interest rates, you may be able to reduce your current payment and lock in an attractive rate for the life of your loan. Those planning to move in a short time, such as five years, may still want to take advantage of the lower rates offered by ARMs.

■ Take advantage of equity in your home by refinancing for more than your current mortgage balance. You can then use the extra money to pay off higher-interest-rate loans, such as car loans and credit card balances.

■ Think about refinancing for a shorter term—perhaps fifteen years instead of thirty years. While that may actually increase your monthly mortgage payment, you'll pay the mortgage off much sooner, saving a significant amount in interest payments.

Protect Your Family's Security

My son and his wife live from paycheck to paycheck. This is not necessary because they both have great jobs. I believe they have no idea how to protect their family in case of a financial emergency. Do you have some tips?

Jewel C. of Hickory, MS

One of your first financial goals should be to protect your family's financial security from catastrophes. To do so, provide for these four items:

1. *A cash reserve for short-term emergencies, such as a temporary job loss, major home repair, or large medical bill.* A common rule of thumb states that your cash reserve should equal two to six months' living expenses. However, how much you'll need depends on your age, health, job outlook, and borrowing capacity. You may need a larger reserve if you expect to be laid off or lose your job, you are the sole wage earner in the family, or your income fluctuates. A smaller reserve may be needed if you have more than one source of family income or you can borrow quickly, such as through a home-equity line of credit.

2. *Adequate insurance in all major areas.* Your insurance needs will change over the years, so you may find yourself with too much or too little coverage. Thus, periodically review your life, disability, medical, and homeowners insurance. Don't overlook disability income insurance, which can be very important if you're unable to work due to an illness or injury.

3. *Umbrella liability insurance to protect against major lawsuits.* Umbrella policies are purchased in $1 million increments and kick in once the limits of your homeowners and automobile policies are exceeded. In addition to the items covered by those policies, an umbrella policy typically covers damages from use of nonowned property in your possession and from lawsuits for libel, slander, defamation of character, and invasion of privacy.

4. *A power of attorney.* A power of attorney gives an individual
you designate the power to act on your behalf when you can't.

Curbing Debt

■ Pay down as much debt as you can. Significant amounts of
debt can seriously threaten your financial security in the
event of a job layoff or major reduction to your income.
Quit incurring new debt and try to pay off as much existing
debt as possible.

■ Cut back on your lifestyle. The amount of money you have
left over for saving is a direct result of your lifestyle. Your
lifestyle decisions will also affect you in the future, since you
probably will want a similar lifestyle after retirement.

■ Find out where your money is going. Analyzing how you
spend your income will help you find ways to reduce
spending. You may be able to refinance your mortgage,
consider new tax strategies, or comparison shop for items
like insurance.

Dealing with Money Issues

*My daughter-in-law spends money like water. She spends her pay-
check on clothes and my son's paycheck on luxuries like jewelry
and a sports car. This weekend he asked me to lend them a couple thousand dollars to pay off some of their debts. Before I do, I
want them to have a road map that will help them to better manage their own money.*

Walter W. of East St. Louis, IL

If married couples don't agree on basic money issues, money matters can be a constant source of conflict. To help your son and his
wife avoid money conflicts, consider giving them these tips:

- Discuss your views on a wide range of money issues, paying particular attention to potential sources of conflict. Make sure you understand each other's views about earning, spending, saving, investing, and borrowing. Does one of you like to save money, while the other prefers to spend it? Does one feel comfortable with high debt levels, while the other can't stand the thought of paying interest? Different money issues will be more important at different stages of your life. Thus, you may find that for years you have no money disagreements, only to be faced with an issue you can't agree on.

- Agree on basic monetary goals and develop a written budget. The process of defining goals and setting a budget can help resolve different views about money matters, by forcing couples to compromise and make decisions about how money will be spent. With the issues resolved and a plan in place, there is less room for disagreement.

- Decide whether you want joint or separate accounts. Some individuals prefer to pool all funds, while others feel uncomfortable losing control of their money. For couples with vastly different spending styles, separate accounts may reduce tension. A joint account can be used for shared expenses, with each spouse contributing a designated amount to the account. Any remaining funds are kept in individual accounts, for each spouse to spend as he or she desires.

- Develop credit in each spouse's name. Each spouse should have separate credit cards to develop his or her own credit file. This can be especially important if one spouse dies or the couple divorces.

- Decide how long-term investment decisions will be made. Women tend to be more conservative investors than men, usually conducting more research before purchase. Utilize these differing styles to develop an investment strategy you both are comfortable with.

- Consider a prenuptial agreement. If you are getting married, you may want to consider a prenuptial agreement to spell out how property will be divided in the event of divorce or death. While many individuals may find this a drastic step, those remarrying, with children from a prior marriage, or with significant assets or a business may want the protection of a prenuptial agreement.

Controlling Consumer Debt

To ensure that credit card debt doesn't become a problem, consider these tips:

- Figure out how burdensome your debt is by calculating your debt ratio. Your debt ratio is your monthly payments (excluding mortgage payments) divided by your monthly net income. Start seriously looking for ways to reduce your debt when that ratio approaches 10 percent to 15 percent of your net income. Consider seeking professional help if your debt ratio is greater than 20 percent. This level of debt can cause serious financial problems if you encounter sudden reductions in your income. Even those with a debt ratio under 10 percent may want to find ways to reduce their debt.

- Use your credit cards only if you can pay the balance in full each month, thus eliminating high interest payments. If you can't do that, at least make sure to pay more than the minimum monthly payment.

- Carry only one or two credit cards to make it easier to monitor your spending. You may want to ask your lender to reduce your credit limit, so you aren't tempted to get into too much debt. Or consider using a debit card, which automatically deducts charges from your bank account.

- Consider transferring credit card balances with high interest rates to lower-rate alternatives. Or call the lender and negotiate a better rate.

- Pay off consumer debt as quickly as possible. Since you don't get a tax deduction for any interest payments, paying off a credit card balance that carries 18 percent interest equates to a 25 percent pretax return for those in the 28 percent tax bracket.

- Apply extra payments to the credit card with the highest interest rate. Once that balance is paid in full, move on to the card with the next-highest interest rate.

- Purchase items on credit only if they will appreciate in value. Forcing yourself to pay cash for other items can significantly reduce your debt load.

- Consider obtaining a home-equity loan to pay off your consumer debt. In most cases, home-equity loan interest rates are lower than rates on other consumer loans. Also, as long as the home-equity loan does not exceed $100,000, interest payments are tax deductible. Use this strategy with care, however, since you don't want to pay off the credit cards and then run up new debts.

What If You Divorce?

My husband and I are getting a divorce. We are roughly $20,000 in debt, not including my car lease. I unfortunately have been left with all the bills with the exception of my husband's car. My debt to income ratio is too high. I have contacted a debt consolidation company in an attempt to pay off my bills. I make enough money that I should be able to clear up this mess in a timely manner. I constantly live paycheck to paycheck and I don't have any savings. If I lost my job today, I would not have a safety net to catch me. I would appreciate any guidance I can get.

Yvette J. of San Diego, CA

I have consulted many resources designed to help you through your situation. My job is to assist people in creating and maintaining their financial portfolios, but from time to time a couple I am working with decides to divorce. Although an investment professional is not a marriage counselor, he or she can be of some help as you plan your divorce.

While generally you will need to have an attorney to handle the legal issues regarding a divorce, your investment professional can play some important roles in the proceedings. An investment professional can provide you with information to help you make decisions about how to divide your property, what the tax implications may be of your options, how to determine what debts you owe, can show you the results of different scenarios so you can make informed choices, and more. Other roles of the investment professional may be:

- *Strategist.* To help you understand the financial implications of your divorce settlement issues.
- *Mediator.* To develop an accurate picture of your financial situation.
- *Negotiator.* To resolve discrepancies over property valuation based on financial research and projections.
- *Client expectations manager.* To prepare you for the realities of your divorce and resultant financial situation.
- *Trial preparation assistant.* To help to optimize the outcome of any trial for you.
- *Evidence presenter.* To explain financial matters in court.

Property Ownership

While not an outcome most of us want to consider when getting married, divorce is a common occurrence today. There are 1.4 million divorces in the United States each year. Nearly 50 percent of first marriages end in divorce, while 60 percent of second marriages do. And with such an emotionally charged event, you'll want to make the financial and legal processes as easy and as quick as possible.

The best way to ensure a relatively smooth divorce, at least financially, is for both parties to be as open as possible about their financial affairs. The more secretive a spouse is about what they own or owe, the longer and more involved the process to uncover assets and/or debts becomes. By coming to an agreement about property and debt, you can often avoid long, drawn-out battles that can add months, or even years, to the divorce process.

There are three major concerns as you begin to divide your property in a divorce:

1. What's mine, yours, and ours?
2. How much is our property worth?
3. How are we going to divide the property?

To determine what your assets are, you and your spouse should put together an overall written inventory of your property. The next step is to determine who owns what. An important categorization when determining ownership is separate versus marital property.

Separate property includes items brought into the marriage, items inherited during the marriage, and items received as gifts during the marriage.

Marital property is everything (besides personal gifts and inheritance) acquired during the marriage, no matter whose name it is in. In some states, any increase in the value of separate property is considered marital property.

After you've determined what you each own separately, you will need to determine a value for your marital property. Sometimes you may choose to keep several pieces together in order to retain the value of an entire set, such as a furniture collection or china. Other items may have an emotional value attached to them that goes beyond their monetary worth. You and your spouse should indicate a value next to each piece of property on your inventory list. For some items you may want to refer to outside sources in order to determine their value.

Some examples include:

■ *House.* You can get a formal appraisal, ask a real-estate agent for the price they would assign to the house, or find out what similar properties are selling for in your neighborhood.

- *Car.* There are reference guides at the library and on the Internet to help you determine the current value of a vehicle. You can also refer to the used-car section of a newspaper to find out the asking prices for vehicles similar to yours or consult car dealerships to see what they would offer.
- *Other items.* If you have to know the original purchase price, you can use that amount to make a decision about the items' current value. In general you should try to avoid fighting over items that are not worth as much as you think they are, such as consumer electronics that tend to depreciate quickly over time.

Property Distribution

The next step is probably the most difficult: determining who gets what. Different states have different laws regarding property distribution. It may be helpful to find out about your state's law (in other words, what each of you would get should you have to take your divorce case before a judge) and use that information as a guide when dividing your marital assets. The two main methods states use are:

1. Community property.

Each spouse's separate property is identified and not distributed by a court. All remaining property is equally distributed.

2. Equitable distribution.

A couple's marital property is distributed equitably, which does not mean equally, but fairly. In other words, the result may not be a fifty-fifty split. The spouse with less savings and earning potential, for example, could be granted more than a 50 percent share.

Nonproperty issues are also considered, such as earning potential, career assets (job benefits: insurance, vacation, Social Security, stock options, and pensions), and personal investments in the marriage (the less tangible choices or sacrifices made on behalf of the couple by one spouse, such as quitting a job or postponing education to take care of the family to allow the other spouse to complete studies or advance in his or her career).

Options for undertaking property distribution on your own include:

- *Taking turns.* Although this may sound like a childhood game of round robin, in this situation you and your spouse take turns choosing an item off your inventory list until all of the property has been distributed.

- *Trading.* You and your spouse create trade agreements based on the relative values you place on your property. For example, one spouse would be willing to trade the furniture and silver in return for the car and appliances.

- *Setting value limits.* Determine a value for each item and what percentage of the total value of all property you and your spouse will receive. Then both of you choose items until your share limits are reached.

- *Splitting profits.* Marital property is sold and the profits divided equally between the two of you.

- *Enlisting a third party.* You can place your case with an arbitrator who will determine how the property should be divided after speaking with you and reviewing the evidence. Or you can consult a mediator who will help you and your spouse work out how to value and divide your property.

In a divorce, debt should be treated like property. If you do not pay off all your debts before the divorce process begins, then you will have to determine who is responsible for each debt, in a fashion similar to how your property was distributed.

- *Individual debt.* This is considered separate property.
- *Joint debt.* This is considered marital property.
- *Debts involving an asset.* These are considered to be the responsibility of the owner of the asset (such as a car loan or mortgage).
- *Debts concerning children.* In general these debts are split equally between the spouses.

It is important to confirm what is actually individual versus joint debt. Just because your name does not appear on a credit card, for example, does not mean you are not responsible for the account. The best strategy may be to order a credit report to determine who "owns" which debts (see below for details on credit agencies).

The length of the divorce process depends, in part, on how much you and your spouse can cooperate with each other, how quickly information is provided, and whether you are able to avoid a court trial. If you do end up going to trial, the length of the divorce process is not easy to predict, as you'll need to schedule hearings with the court in your state.

Resources for Further Information

To find out the fair market value of your home, visit Acxiom Property Data and Services at http://products.dataquick.com/consumer and purchase a Home Sales Report or get a free Home Sale Price Trends report about your neighborhood.

To find out the value of your automobiles, refer to the Kelley Blue Book at your local library or visit www.kbb.com.

To purchase credit reports, contact these agencies:

Equifax: 1-800-685-1111 or www.equifax.com

Experion (formerly TRW): 1-800-392-1122 or www.experion.com

TransUnion: 1-800-916-8800 or www.tuc.com

The American Bar Association offers tables summarizing state laws on their Web site at www.abanet.org/family/familylaw.

Visit these Web sites for information on divorce:

www.divorceinfo.com: covers most aspects of divorce

www.divorcenet.com: offers a state-by-state resource directory

Chapter 3

Face the Future

Financial Overview

I am a widow who just married for the second time. For the past three years I have invested $50 per month. I need to increase my investment and figure out how to make sure I have enough money to support myself if something happens to my new husband.

Mable C. of Lexington, VA

Take a time-out to review your investment targets and determine whether or not your investments are meeting your financial goals.

This financial overview will help you see where you should reposition assets in order to continue to work toward your goals.

Also, keep in mind that you should be investing regularly to meet your needs for the future. Even if you can invest only a small amount of money, please do it.

> **TIP** No matter what type of financial plan you have, its success generally will depend on what you put into it.

Financial Fitness

I have been investing the same amount of money every month for the past several years. During that time I received periodic reports about how my money is faring. Thus far, I have seen more downward movement than upward movement. This is not good!

Elaine H. of Lynchburg, VA

How healthy are you? You may be relieved to find out that I mean financially, not physically. In order to be healthy physically we need to have a plan for diet and exercise and consistently strive to meet our goals. Financial health works the same way.

Our financial plan is like our diet and exercise program. We need to be monitoring our progress and ensuring that we stick to our diet (financial plan).

Just as exercising is easier with a partner, managing your money may also be easier when you have someone there

> **TIP** Our goals are long-term in nature, so if we get off track at times, such as not saving one month, we can make up for it by getting back on the program.

to monitor your progress and encourage you along the way. That's what financial advisers do. They are trained to help you design a financial plan, follow it, and strive to meet your goals. That's why you need to meet with one regularly, so she or he can "coach" you and encourage you to stay on track.

As you know, it is often a long time before you see the effects of a healthy lifestyle. Financially this is true, too. Many of the goals you have are probably long-term, such as paying for your children's college education or funding a retirement full of travel. You will be able to see the potential benefits of following your financial plan if you hang in there for the long haul.

Perhaps your top priority is to meet your financial goals. You can do that by creating a financial plan that you can stick with so that you will have the money to enjoy life now and in the future. Once you have a plan in place and follow it, you should monitor it regularly to ensure that it keeps pace with your changing needs.

Financial Checklist

Most people already keep a list of appointments, of errands to run, chores to finish, presents to buy, and places to go.
Now here is the best list you will ever have!

- Prepare a net worth statement as of January 1 to give yourself a snapshot of your current financial position.
- Prepare another statement at the end of the year to see how much progress you made during the year.
- Create a budget to guide your spending for the year.
- Update your financial plan.
- Get in the habit of saving by setting aside a set amount each week.
- Review your investment portfolio to ensure that it matches your asset allocation goals.
- Look for ways to reduce your total debt or to reduce the cost of your borrowing.
- If you have a school-age child, set up a college fund.
- Review your employer's total benefit program, ensuring that you are utilizing all appropriate benefits.
- Invest in retirement plans available through your employer.
- Review your tax situation, looking for ways to reduce your annual taxes.
- Review your insurance coverage.
- Update your will and estate plan.

Maintaining a Long-Term Focus

I admit that I don't know the difference between a bear and a bull. I do know that one of them is responsible for me not earning money on my investments last year. Obviously I need a change, but where do I turn for advice?

Samuel P. of Phoenix, AZ

Alast year was a difficult year for most investors—the stock and bond markets were very volatile. While most of us realize intellectually that we must assume greater risk in order to achieve higher returns, emotionally it is often difficult to continue investing when the future direction of the markets is unclear.

In this type of environment, the guidance of a knowledgeable adviser can help you stay the course. This is an excellent time to reevaluate your investments and objectives.

It is critical, now more than ever, that your investment strategy matches your goals and objectives.

Chapter 4

Check Up on Insurance

Insurance Apprehension

When we think of insurance, it often brings to mind many unpopular ideas. We consider the tragedy we would rather avoid, or we cringe at the thought of reading a complicated policy.

Although insurance may be a dreaded subject, it is an important part of your financial plan. In some cases, insurance can be fairly straightforward. For example, if you want to drive a car or own a house, you need auto or homeowners insurance. Insurance gets tricky when owning the policy is discretionary. There are a myriad of policies and coverage levels, which can become overwhelming. At that point, rather than sifting through the information, it becomes easier to put it off for another time.

TIP It is essential to have proper insurance. Don't wait for a tragedy to discover you are not covered or that the coverage you selected is inadequate.

How Much Is Enough?

My father has insurance policies for his life, health, car, house, and death. Now he has bought another life insurance policy. Enough!

Jonathan E. of Decatur, MS

In order to make sure your family is adequately protected, it's important that you purchase the proper amount of life insurance. A common rule of thumb is that you should purchase five to seven times your annual income. Unfortunately, like most rules of thumb, this does not take into account individual circumstances and may leave you with an inadequate amount of insurance.

The amount of insurance you need depends on your current net worth, the lifestyle you want to provide for your family, and ultimately, your personal desires. First, you should consider how much your family will need every year, being sure to take into account the effects of inflation.

Next, total your assets and other sources of family income. Be sure to include any benefits your family may be entitled to under any pension plans. If your spouse doesn't work now, you need to consider if he or she would work if you died and how much he or she could earn. Don't overlook Social Security survivors' benefits available to your children under age eighteen and to your spouse if he or she does not earn significant wages.

Finally, determine how much life insurance you require. This will depend on how long your family will need this income, what rate of return can be earned on the insurance proceeds, and other factors.

Unfortunately, this is not a calculation that can be made only once. Since your needs change over time, you should assess your insurance coverage periodically, especially if a major event occurs in your life.

Make Sure You're Covered

I am buying a house. My sister told me that when she bought her house, she also bought disability insurance. Why would I need this extra insurance?

Tom W. of Albany, NY

Although a person under age sixty-five is more likely to become disabled than to die, most people assume that life insurance is a more significant need than disability income insurance. However, we suggest that you take a few moments to reconsider.

In many cases, without insurance, you and your family would have to liquidate savings and sell your assets to cover expenses.

Don't assume that Social Security benefits will relieve this need. The criteria to qualify for benefits are stringent, and benefits are modest.

The cost of disability income insurance depends on several factors, including your age, health, and occupation. Make certain that the policy covers you appropriately. Group policies often are not sufficient for your needs, but can be combined with personal policies. If cost is a factor, you can reduce the premium by extending the waiting period before benefits begin.

Life Insurance: One Step at a Time

I know I need life insurance, but how can I tell the difference between the various types? Which one is right for me?

Faye W. of Gulfport, MS

Are you confused by the prospect of purchasing life insurance? The process can be more manageable if you approach it step by step. The first step is to think through some issues that would affect your insurance needs, such as:

- What are your financial goals?
- How much would your family need to live on if you died?
- How much do you want to pay for life insurance?
- What expenses would be incurred if you were sick and needed special care?
- What debts (mortgage, taxes, etc.) would need to be paid after your death?

Once you have answered these questions, the next step is to evaluate the different types of life insurance to determine which is best for your situation. The two main types of life insurance are term and cash-value.

With term insurance, you purchase insurance protection only, with none of the premium set aside to build cash value. Your beneficiary receives the policy proceeds if you die during the policy's term, but you get nothing if the policy is canceled. Some term policies are convertible, allowing you to transfer to a cash-value policy at a later date. Any term life insurance policies you are considering should be renewable regardless of changes in your health.

Cash-value insurance accumulates, from premiums paid and from investment earnings, a cash surrender value that is your property. If you surrender the policy, you receive the cash surrender value. Furthermore, you can borrow on the cash value through a policy loan, but any outstanding loans are subtracted from the insurance proceeds when you die. A wide variety of cash-value insurance policies exist, with numerous riders available to meet specific needs.

Planning for Your Family's Financial Future

My uncle is an independent contractor. He just got hurt on a job, and we discovered that he will not be able to work for at least a year. Unfortunately, if he cannot work, he cannot pay his mortgage. I, too, am an independent contractor. How can I safeguard my house if something like this happens to me?

Etherine J. of Buckhead, GA

If you are like many people, you get up every day, eat breakfast, get in your car, and go to work. We take these things for granted—a place to live, food to eat, a car to drive, and most important, our ability to work. Imagine for a minute what would happen if you were disabled and couldn't work. How would your family survive without your income? What would happen to the assets you've worked so hard to accumulate?

Although we don't want to spend our lives worrying about becoming disabled, we should consider the ramifications if that should happen. The odds of suffering a long-term disability at some time during your life are 44 percent at age twenty-five, 42 percent at age thirty, 41 percent at age thirty-five, 39 percent at age forty, 36 percent at age forty-five, 33 percent at age fifty, and 27 percentat age fifty-five (Source: General Electric Capital Assurance Company). Therefore, you should plan ahead to help ensure your family will be secure financially if you're unable to work.

The cost of disability income protection varies depending on a number of factors, including your age, occupation, and benefits. Don't hesitate to plan for your family's financial future.

Do You Need Long-Term-Care Insurance?

My job has offered me long-term-care insurance. Mother says I should take it, but it is another insurance fee that I can see no use for. Why would I need this?

Paul R. of Gary, IN

Why do you buy auto insurance? Most people buy auto insurance to protect them if they get in an accident or their car is stolen. Even though we don't want these things to happen, we want to be prepared financially. Long-term-care insurance works the same way. None of us plan on becoming ill, but statistics show that many people need nursing home or at-home care sometime in their lives. Long-term-care insurance provides a way to pay for this care. The life span of the average African American is longer and longer these days.

Even if you've planned for retirement, you may have neglected to think about health-care costs. Since many health insurance policies do not cover the cost of long-term care, many people are forced to pay the expenses out of their pockets. Medicare has very strict rules that must be met before they will pay for long-term care, and even then, benefits are only payable for the first one hundred days.

When you think about a long-term-care policy, you need to consider your net worth, the potential cost of long-term care, and the cost of the policy. Since women typically live longer than men, they are more likely to need long-term care. Children may want to consider long-term-care insurance for their parents. Most adult children would take care of a parent if the need arose, but it could become a burden on their lives and finances. A long-term-care policy can take care of the money aspects. Most policies can also pay for a nursing home stay or for care at home.

Because of the nature of long-term-care insurance, the longer you wait, the more expensive the policy becomes. If you wait until you actually need coverage, it will likely be too late to obtain it.

Fast Facts on Long-Term-Care Insurance

My fifty-year-old father just purchased long-term-care insurance. I am frightened that this means he has an illness that he is not admitting. But he says this is a normal purchase for a man in his position. Why?

Janice J. of Cincinnati, OH

Do you know what long-term-care insurance is? Do you know why you might need it? Here are some facts to help you learn about this valuable tool:

- Long-term-care insurance can help protect you financially from the high costs of custodial and/or nursing home care during retirement.
- Policies that cover most types of care (e.g., at-home care, nursing home care) are most beneficial to you, since they can

be tailored to your situation and needs. It is important to make sure your policy covers several types of care, including custodial care in residential facilities, adult day care, and home health care.

- You can buy policies with different deductible periods, inflation protection, and varying coverage.
- Premium costs vary, depending on what type of coverage you choose and at what age you buy the policy. It can be beneficial to buy long-term-care insurance when you are in your mid-fifties or your sixties and still in good health. If you wait until your health is deteriorating, you may have a hard time getting coverage or be forced to pay very high premiums.
- Policies have differing requirements as to when coverage starts. Most policies will start paying when you are unable to perform two or three basic living activities. Make sure you don't choose a policy that requires you to be totally incapacitated before benefits are paid.
- Any policy you choose should be issued by a company with a strong history of satisfied customers and strict underwriting requirements.

If you would like more information about long-term-care insurance and how it applies to your situation, please contact a professional.

Life Insurance Mistakes African Americans Don't Want to Make

My late husband and I thought we were doing all the right things. We bought life insurance policies that would take care of our burial expenses and leave a little extra for our kids. Unfortunately, we did not know the difference between whole life and term life and did not realize that we should have paid more attention to the value of the policy. What went wrong?

Gertrude J. of Columbia, SC

Aere are the five most common mistakes people make when buying life insurance:

1. Purchasing life insurance based on face amount rather than income needs. Make sure you look at the income your heirs will be able to generate from the policy and that it is adequate for their needs.

2. Neglecting to review your life insurance policies regularly. It is important to review your policies at least every other year to make sure everything is up-to-date and that your beneficiaries are correct.

3. Naming your estate as your beneficiary. If you do this, the proceeds (in most states) will be subject to state inheritance taxes, probate costs, and claims of creditors. This leaves little for your true heirs.

4. Failing to name contingent beneficiaries. Not only do you need to name a primary beneficiary, you should name contingent beneficiaries. If you don't do this, the proceeds from your insurance will be paid to your estate and will be subject to the expenses mentioned in mistake 3.

5. Buying the wrong product for your situation. There are basically four types of life insurance: term, permanent, universal, and variable. The policies in the marketplace today are variations or combinations of these four basic types. Because it can be so confusing, make sure you use a professional who understands your situation and will help you choose the product that best meets your needs.

Do You Need Life Insurance?

I think a life insurance policy is a waste of time. It does me no good when I die, so why buy one?

Carla B. of Memphis, TN

Think for a minute about what you need in life. Food, clothing, and shelter top the list. What about that nice car or comfortable home?

How about life insurance? As American Express says, "Don't leave home without it." African Americans need life insurance.

Many of the things we have are not necessities. We could get by without a big home or closet full of clothes, but these things are little extras that we enjoy. In the same way, life insurance is not an absolute necessity. If you didn't have life insurance, you would probably still have a funeral and your family would somehow manage to live without your income. However, since you have the chance to plan for a comfortable future for your family, why not do it? A new father may not be alive to see his child graduate from college, but he can still plan for that to happen by creating a college fund.

Life insurance is meant to provide a comfortable lifestyle for your family if you die. You don't want to leave them with a large mortgage, other debt, or a large estate tax bill. Life insurance gives you another chance to show your family how much you love them by taking care of these things in advance.

Although you can see no immediate benefits from life insurance, it is a way to help others accomplish things even if you're not around to witness these events. No, you don't need life insurance, but it's a little "extra" in life that will help should the need arise.

What If?

Life is good! I live in a nice condo, drive a luxury automobile, just met the woman of my dreams, and landed a huge account at work. Plus, my daughter just got accepted into one of the best colleges in the Midwest. What more do I need?

Wallace D. of Oak Park, IL

What if one day you are driving to work, thinking about how great your family is and how well business is going, when you get hit by another car? Your car is totaled, you can't think clearly, and then you feel the pain in your legs. On your way to the hospital, all you can think about is how you will provide for your family. What will happen while you recover? How will you pay the hospital bills?

Hopefully this won't happen to you. However, accidents happen and serious health problems confront thousands of people every day. How can you prepare for something like this?

The answer is disability insurance. You may think that you just need life insurance, but the likelihood of becoming disabled is greater than you may think. For instance, a twenty-year-old has a 30 percent chance of becoming disabled for some period during his or her lifetime. One of the greatest assets you have is your ability to earn an income. If that is taken away from you, how will you pay for daily expenses, as well as those related to your disability?

If your current assets cannot support you and your family until you are sixty-five, you need to think about disability insurance and incorporate it into your financial plans. Studies show that African Americans do this far less than any other group of people.

Reasons to Own Life Insurance

I have spent most of my fifty years on welfare. When welfare reform came, I got a job and after a while realized that I am good at it. My boss recently told me that I should buy some life insurance. Why?

Kissie L. of Gary, IN

Why is it that so many African Americans do not think about life insurance? Life insurance is something we don't like to think about, but it does have many useful purposes. Here are several reasons that it may be a good idea to own life insurance:

- To create an estate. Sometimes we are not able to save as much as we would like to leave to our heirs. By owning life insurance, however, you may be able to leave a sizable estate to your loved ones.
- To pay estate taxes and other settlement costs upon death. These costs can be substantial, sometimes as much as 50 percent of the estate or more. Owning a life insurance policy

gives your heirs a means by which to pay these expenses without worrying where the money will come from.

- To fund a business transfer. Often partners in a business will agree to buy out a deceased owner's share from his or her estate upon death. Life insurance could provide cash for this transaction.
- To provide a college education for children or grandchildren. Increases in the cash value of a policy on a minor's life (or the parent's life) can be used to accumulate funds for college.
- To accumulate a nest egg for your retirement. There are many insurance products that offer competitive returns. This could be a good way for you to save money to fund your retirement.
- To even up inheritances. You may have a family business that you are passing on to children who are active in the business. You may also have other children who are not active in the business, but who you would still like to receive an inheritance. Life insurance provides a way to give equal amounts to all your children.

Evaluating Your Life Insurance Needs

My children have more money than I ever earned in my entire lifetime. So it seems to me that a simple life insurance policy that can bury me would be sufficient.

Sarah S. of Lexington, KY

We are often asked how to determine the appropriate amount of insurance coverage. The answer, of course, varies by client and circumstance. The amount a young couple with one child may need is often quite different from that needed by an established family of five or an older, wealthy couple desiring to protect their estate.

Before deciding how much you need, there are two questions you need to ask yourself. Will there be a point where your death will cause a financial loss? If so, do you want to prevent that loss? For instance, a married couple with plans to start a family in a few years may want to plan as though the children have already been born. A medical resident or young attorney may want to provide coverage to assure a standard of living he or she is working toward but may not achieve for several years.

Your Insurance Needs Depend on Your Stage in Life

When my kids were younger, I kept enough life insurance to make sure they would not be a financial burden on my relatives. Now that they are adults, I want to turn my attention to my retirement. Is this wrong?

Wanda J. of Glendale, CA

When was the last time you looked at your life insurance policy? As an African American, you should review your insurance needs periodically because the types of coverage you require as well as the amount you need will change as you reach different stages in your life.

For example, if you're young and single, you might not need life insurance because you have no dependents. On the other hand, if you have children and your spouse doesn't work, you will probably need significant amounts of insurance. If you're older, have no children, and have a modest estate, you might not need life insurance, but you might benefit from long-term-care insurance in the event of a nursing-home stay.

When assessing your insurance requirements—what kinds and how much you need—you must first identify and analyze all

> **FYI**
>
> You may want less coverage in one area because you have other assets that can cover that expense. Only a periodic review of your current situation will make sure that you have the right type of coverage in the proper amounts. ■

the possible risks you face. Then you must decide how much risk you are willing to take on yourself and how much insurance you need to cover risks you don't want to assume.

Life Insurance Can Fund Many Needs

My husband and I are living with his mom and are trying to save for a house. My mother-in-law just told me that I can borrow against my life insurance policy to get the down payment. Is this true, or is she just trying to get rid of us?

Cheri J. of Houston, TX

Many African Americans think life insurance's most common purpose is to ensure that one's family can maintain their current standard of living in the event of the insured's death. But life insurance can also be used to help fund other needs.

- You can borrow against your life insurance to make a down payment on a house.
- By taking out extra amounts of insurance, an insured can provide the means to pay for a child's education or to pay off a mortgage or other debts.
- Life insurance can be used to leave a substantial inheritance to your heirs or to fund a large charitable gift.
- Life insurance is often used to provide the funds to pay estate taxes upon the insured's death. If properly structured, the life insurance proceeds can be both income-tax and estate-tax free.
- Business owners often obtain life insurance to ensure that the business will not be sold to pay estate and inheritance taxes or as a means to fund a buy-sell agreement.

Review Your Policies Annually

I have had homeowners insurance for the past twelve years. Last winter, my basement flooded and I discovered that nothing in my policy covered this. What should I do to make sure I don't get caught again?

Sandra G. of Stone Mountain, GA

Do your insurance policies provide you with adequate protection in all major areas, including life, health, disability, homeowners or renters, automobile, and personal liability? When was the last time you reviewed all of your insurance policies?

Your insurance needs do not remain stagnant and will change over time. You should assess your insurance coverage periodically, especially if a major event occurs. Having another child, getting married, obtaining a large salary increase, moving to a new house—all of these events can alter your insurance needs drastically.

Insuring Your Prized Possession

I came home from work yesterday and discovered that a tree had fallen through the roof of my house directly into my bedroom. When I called my insurance agent, he started to explain why some of the replacement charges would be covered while others would not. It is obvious that I need to change my coverage—but how?

Jenny L. of Fort Wayne, IN

To many African Americans, the most valuable asset they own is their home. Since homeowners insurance protects one of your most valuable assets, you should know the answers to the following questions:

What types of damages are covered? Basic policies protect you from fire, smoke, windstorms, vandalism, and lightning. The most comprehensive policies cover every peril except those specifically excluded, generally floods, earthquakes, war, and nuclear accidents. Protection from these perils may require special policies.

How much coverage should you obtain? A general rule is to insure your home for at least 80 percent of its replacement value, since homes are seldom completely destroyed. Many people, however, feel more comfortable insuring their home for 100 percent of its replacement value. To keep your policy limits up-to-date, either check with your agent annually or obtain an inflation endorsement, which increases your policy limits in accordance with changes in residential construction costs.

Are personal possessions covered? Your policy also covers your personal property for a maximum of 50 percent of the coverage on your home. However, your policy probably pays actual cash value, meaning depreciation will be charged against the amount you paid for the property. For an additional premium, you can obtain a replacement cost endorsement that pays an amount sufficient to replace your property. Most policies have low limits for jewelry, watches, silverware, furs, and collectibles, so you may need additional insurance for these items.

What other items are covered by your homeowners insurance? Your policy probably also covers some additional items, including loss or damage to personal property while away from home; extra living expenses if your home is damaged; other people's property that you damage; damage to your trees, shrubs, and lawn; and your liability for fraudulent charges to your credit cards. Ensure that the limits for personal liability coverage are adequate. Your policy probably doesn't cover business activities, so if someone in your family works at home even part-time, you should consider adding an incidental business option to your policy.

Review Your Insurance Needs

Several years ago, I purchased insurance polices to cover many different contingencies. I believe they are still good—is it necessary to go through all of the hassle to make sure?

Dorothy M. of Detroit, MI

At least annually, you should review your insurance coverage in the following areas:

- *Life insurance.* The primary purpose of life insurance is to ensure that, in the event of your death, your family has adequate resources to maintain their current lifestyle. Life insurance can

FACTORS TO CONSIDER BEFORE PURCHASING A DISABILITY POLICY

- *Character of the company.* When selecting an insurer, look for a quality company with a good reputation and high ratings.

- *Renewability clause.* Select a policy that has a "noncancelable and guaranteed renewable" clause. That means that as long as you pay the premiums, which will remain fixed, the policy cannot be canceled.

- *Elimination period.* This is the length of time that you must be disabled before benefits will start. Your waiting period should be based on your employer's sick-leave policy and your own cash reserves.

- *Benefit period.* This is the length of time that the policy will continue to pay benefits.

- *Definition of disability.* This is one of the most important aspects of a disability policy. Three of the most common definitions include: not being able to engage in your "own occupation"; not being able to perform any occupation; or being confined to your home.

- *Cost.* While cost is always important, it is more important to ensure that the policy is appropriate for your circumstances.

---

also serve other purposes, such as providing liquidity to an estate or enabling business partners to buy out the heirs of a deceased partner.

TIP It is highly recommended that your life insurance coverage be reviewed once a year.

- *Health insurance.* Don't assume that your health insurance is adequate. Investigate your coverage to see if you need supplemental protection.

- *Disability insurance.* Disability insurance pays you a monthly income if you are unable to work because of illness or injury. The economic consequences of disability are usually severe. Not only is your income reduced or eliminated for a period of time, but you will probably also incur higher costs for medical and personal care.

■ *Homeowners and renters insurance.* In addition to protecting your home, most homeowners policies also cover your household furnishings, personal liability if someone is hurt on your property, personal property taken with you while away from home, extra living expenses if your home is damaged, other people's property that you damage, damage to landscaping, and your liability for fraudulent charges on your credit cards.

■ *Automobile insurance.* While most states require some auto insurance, most drivers elect to increase that coverage.

■ *Personal liability insurance.* This covers you once the liability limits of your automobile and homeowners policies have been exceeded. It also covers risks not included in other policies, such as claims against you for libel, slander, invasion of privacy, or defamation of character.

> **TIP** Since your needs will change over time, review your policies at least annually. If there is a major change in your life, such as a job change or marriage, review your coverage immediately.

Here are just a few of the reasons you should conduct an annual insurance review: if you haven't looked over your personal insurance policies in over a year, if you don't own an umbrella policy, if you don't know if your premiums are reasonable, and if you think you might be underinsured in an area. If you don't, your family will ultimately pay the price.

Before Purchasing Insurance

Three years ago I purchased life, auto, and homeowners insurance from what I thought was an up-and-coming reputable agency. Recently I heard rumors that the owner of this company

---

Managing the Risks in Your Life

In addition to accumulating wealth, you need to ensure that your wealth is adequately protected from the risks we all face in life—death, damage to property, serious illness, loss of income, theft of property. Any one of these disasters can result in significant financial loss. Follow these four steps to manage risk:

1. Identify, analyze, and measure possible risks.

2. Consider all possible risks to your life, health, property, earning capacity, and financial assets.

3. Prepare a property inventory, listing all your assets and their value.

4. Monitor your risk management program periodically. Changes in your personal circumstances will necessitate changes in how you deal with certain risks.

---

had embezzled funds. Obviously I have lost my money. Before I start over with another agency, I need some rules.

Reggie M. of Riverside, IL

Before purchasing insurance, you should carefully evaluate the insurance company. Consumers purchase insurance with the assumption that they will receive benefits at some point in the future—in most cases, sometime in the very distant future. Thus, it is important to be sure that the insurance company is properly managed and financially stable.

It is prudent to invest with a high-quality company. Important measures of quality include the ratings assigned by rating organizations such as A.M. Best, Standard & Poor's, Moody's Investor Services, and Duff & Phelps. In the past, these ratings were primarily designed to measure a company's claims-paying ability. Recently, however, the ratings agencies have been paying more attention to investment risk.

You should also review in depth the investments held by the

insurance company. You should conduct as thorough a review as you would if you were investigating a mutual fund. *Best's Insurance Reports Life-Health,* published annually, provides detailed summaries on insurance company investments for 1,400 companies.

By checking the financial stability of the insurance company before you purchase insurance, you will help ensure that the company will be there when you need it.

Life Insurance Can Fund Many Needs

My mother gave me a life insurance policy that she bought for me and my baby eight years ago. She said that I could borrow against it to pay for my tuition to junior college. I was amazed to find out that this was true.

Cia B. of Oakland, CA

Life insurance is often associated with its most common purpose: to ensure that one's family can maintain their current standard of living in the event of the insured's death. But life insurance can also be used to help fund other needs, and it can be structured to accomplish a number of different objectives.

Protect Your Earning Power

I just had a scare. While working on a client's roof, I fell off. Fortunately, there was a massive shrub that broke my fall, so I was completely unharmed. But it started me to thinking. How would I be able to pay my medical bills and living expenses if I was forced to be off work for an extended period of time?

Marvin C. of Kingston, NY

Most of us have car insurance, homeowners insurance, medical insurance, and life insurance. But how many have insured our most valuable asset of all—our earning power? Long-term-disability insurance is an important component in adequately protecting your family's financial well-being.

There is a full line of disability products that are appropriate for almost any situation—from individual to group coverage, from blue collar to professional coverage. ∎

If your employer provides disability insurance, be sure to review the policy carefully. In most cases, employers provide only short-term disability. You can't count on Social Security to replace your income. To collect benefits, you must be totally disabled, have little or no chance of recovery, and wait six months or longer for your first check. Even if you do qualify, benefits are very modest.

Most of us would not want to deplete our savings for retirement or our children's college education to survive during a long-term disability. Thus, it is important to ensure that you have adequate long-term-disability insurance.

Avoid These Life Insurance Mistakes

My buddy died and left a hefty life insurance policy. He assumed everything would be divided equally between his wife and kids. Turns out his wife never liked her stepkids and kept everything. She said there wasn't enough money to divide. What should he have done to avoid this?

Franklin O. of Portland, OR

Life insurance can be used for a variety of personal and estate planning needs. To make sure that your insurance policy meets your needs, avoid these mistakes:

- ∎ Relying on rules of thumb to calculate your insurance needs. Since everyone's situation is different, you should prepare a detailed analysis.
- ∎ Not considering all types of insurance policies. You should understand the basics of each type before deciding which is most appropriate for you.

- Not selecting the appropriate policy owner. If the policy is properly structured, the proceeds should be paid to your beneficiaries without paying federal income or gift taxes and the proceeds should not be included in your taxable estate.

- Not selecting appropriate beneficiaries. You need to consider the tax ramifications before selecting beneficiaries. For instance, naming your estate as the beneficiary would result in the proceeds being included in your taxable estate. Or, if your spouse owns a policy on your life and your children are listed as beneficiaries, the policy proceeds may be considered a gift, subject to gift taxes.

- Purchasing cash-value insurance for short-term needs. Cash values typically accumulate at a faster rate after the first few years. Thus, you should not consider a cash-value policy unless you're willing to own the policy for at least ten years.

- Not reviewing the insurance company's financial situation. Life insurance proceeds typically won't be paid for years or even decades. Thus, you need to evaluate the financial soundness of the insurance company.

- Replacing an existing life insurance policy without first evaluating the policy. Look at an in-force ledger statement to determine the policy's current status and growth projections. If you need more insurance, you can always apply for another policy for the additional amount needed. A policy change may require a medical examination and may incur fees and costs.

- Not evaluating your situation periodically. Your life insurance needs are likely to change over time. Thus, you should periodically review your needs to see if changes are warranted.

Insuring Your Home

I just refinanced my house. Should I update my homeowners policy, too?

Mary Sue H. of Reno, NV

Take time periodically to review your homeowners insurance policy. Some items to consider include:

- Review the adequacy of your policy limits. Investigate how much it would cost to replace your home, and make sure your policy limits will cover that amount. Try to obtain guaranteed replacement-cost coverage, where the insurance company will rebuild your home even when the cost exceeds the policy limits. Be aware, however, that some companies no longer offer this coverage and even those that do define guaranteed replacement cost in different ways. Some companies will rebuild your home no matter what the cost, while others cap their coverage based on a certain percentage of the policy's face value. Make sure your policy has an inflation endorsement that increases your coverage annually for increases in construction costs.

- Obtain coverage for special risks. Basic policies protect you from fire, smoke, windstorms, vandalism, and lightning. The most comprehensive policies cover every peril except those specifically excluded, typically floods, earthquakes, war, and nuclear accidents. If you live near a floodplain or earthquake area, obtain specific coverage for these hazards.

- Understand what other items are covered by your policy. Your homeowners policy also typically covers personal property, other structures on your property, landscaping, loss of use when your property is destroyed, and personal liability coverage. Carefully review the limits for all of these items, since you can generally add endorsements if you need additional coverage. Typical policies cover personal property for a maximum of 50 percent of the coverage on the home, usually paying actual cash value, which deducts depreciation from the amount paid. Try to obtain a replacement-cost endorsement, which pays to replace your property and typically raises the limit to 70 percent of your home's coverage. Pay special attention to limits for items like jewelry, antiques, collectibles, and works of art.

Managing Life's Risks

I just married the man of my dreams. My mother told me that my husband and I should sit down and make plans as soon as possible for financial emergencies. If I do that, maybe he will think that I am a gold digger. Please help me explain why this talk is needed now.

Catherine C. of Urbana, IL

The goal of risk management is to help you protect your wealth from risks such as death, serious illness, income loss, property damage, and theft. Following these four steps can help you decide how to manage the risks in your life:

1. Identify and measure all possible risks.

Consider risks to your life, health, earning capacity, property, and financial assets. Prepare a property inventory, listing all assets and their value. This will help you determine how much insurance is needed and can help establish proof of loss in the event of a claim. Be aware of items that must be specially insured, such as jewelry, coin collections, antiques, works of art, and the like. Also inventory your activities for possible sources of uninsured liability, which could include incidental business activities or rental property management.

2. Select a risk management technique for each risk.

It would be very expensive to insure for every risk you are subject to, so you may decide to use other strategies for some risks. The primary ways to manage risk include:

- *Avoid the risk.* There are some risks that insurance companies won't insure or that are very expensive to insure. Thus, your best strategy may be to simply avoid the risk. Some examples would include not building a home near a floodplain, not participating in dangerous sports, and not smoking.
- *Reduce the risk.* In many cases, you can reduce the possibility of loss through active steps on your part. For example, you can start exercising, install an alarm system, or wear seat belts.

■ *Retain the risk.* When the cost of insuring the risk exceeds the benefits you would receive, your best option may be to retain the risk. For example, you might not want to purchase extended warranty insurance on small appliances. The use of deductibles and coinsurance are also forms of retaining risk.

■ *Transfer the risk.* Typically, this involves purchasing insurance and is used for major risks that can't be eliminated through risk reduction or avoidance. You should consider insuring all potentially severe losses, such as death, disability, catastrophic health-care costs, major property loss, and personal liability suits.

When examining your risks, consider retaining those with small economic costs while transferring those with large economic costs. Your decision should be based on the amount of the possible loss, not your perception of how likely the event is to occur. For example, many people fail to obtain disability income insurance because they think there is little risk that they will become disabled. Yet a long-term disability can be financially devastating, making it prudent to insure against this risk.

3. Implement your chosen risk management techniques.

Once you decide how to deal with each risk, follow through and implement those techniques.

4. Review your risk management program periodically.

Changes in your personal situation may make it necessary to change how you handle certain risks. For instance, when you are single, you may have little need for life insurance since no one is dependent on your earnings. But once you start a family, life insurance may become very important.

Chapter 5

Trouble-Free Taxes

Tax Time Approaches

Man! They say the only things that are certain are death and taxes. This year, they may become one and the same for me. If you tell me how to avoid one, it will help me delay the other.

Matthew S. of Portland, OR

One of the most unpopular times of the year is tax time. After basking in the warm glow of the holidays, many of us see tax time as an unwelcome but inevitable reality check. During this annual process, you may need an adviser to educate you on the options available.

Tax preparation is not the same as tax planning, though many people confuse the two. Tax preparation is the flurry of last-minute receipt grabbing and scribbling that most people go through. Planning is an ongoing process, one that begins anew each year. Throughout the year, look ahead and plan with ways to help you reduce your tax bill. Can you make a $3,000 contribution to an individual retirement account (IRA) for you and your spouse? Should you purchase a tax-exempt or tax-deferred investment? Are you contributing to your 401(k) plan? These questions, among many others, form the basis for a tax plan.

Tax Planning Leads to Tax Savings

I just got audited for the third year in a row. The auditor felt sorry for me, so he told me to avoid another potential audit by sitting down and developing a tax plan. Are there any strategies that you can share that would help?

Shalinda H. of Fairfax, VA

If you haven't actively followed a yearlong tax plan, you may have paid more than you needed to in income taxes.

The goal of every taxpayer should be to take full advantage of all the legal methods available to reduce his or her tax liability. Remember, effective tax planning takes into consideration the various tax alternatives before completing a transaction. This is one of the areas in which a tax professional can be of service to you.

TIP If you have a desire to reduce your taxes or to discuss investment tax strategies, please contact a professional.

STRATEGIES TO HELP REDUCE YOUR TAXES

- Pay state taxes before year-end to maximize deductions.
- Prepay your second property tax installment.
- Prepay January's mortgage payment.
- Change personal interest to fully deductible home mortgage interest.
- Defer bonuses and compensation until January.
- Sell property on the installment method.

The Time for Year-End Tax Strategies Is Now

The tax man cometh! Maybe not for a couple of months yet. But I need to know how to keep him from taking the shirt off my back when he gets here.

Maryann F. of Little Rock, AR

For most people, the fourth quarter is a good time to consider year-end tax strategies. By implementing a tax strategy, you can gain additional flexibility you might not enjoy if you wait until late December.

Some examples of tax strategies include: selling securities to match capital gains against capital losses, implementing and contributing to a retirement plan, contributing to an IRA, and giving appreciated assets to charities or to other individuals.

Of course, there are many other ways to help you reduce your taxes, and not all of them are available or appropriate for everyone. While it is important to reduce your tax burden, moves made primarily for tax reasons may not be in your overall best interest. It is important to remain focused on your long-term strategies. For example, taxable investments may earn a better return than tax-free investments even after taxes, and some tax strategies may have a negative effect on other aspects of your financial picture.

Avoiding Tax Penalties

Last year, I rushed off to get my taxes done, only to find out that I owed the IRS money because I did not take out enough money for taxes. I want to know what steps I can take to avoid penalties.

John F. of Sacramento, CA

No one likes to pay income taxes, but how would you like to pay penalties on top of those taxes? A large percentage of penalties result from improper payment of estimated taxes, so it is crucial to understand those rules.

Who pays estimated taxes? Estimated tax payments are required if your tax liability will be $1,000 or more above the amount withheld from your salary. Generally, individuals who receive significant income from sources not subject to withholding, such as dividends, interest, capital gains, self-employment income, rent, alimony, partnership interests, and S corporation interests, must make estimated tax payments.

Currently, individuals with adjusted gross income (AGI) over $150,000 in the preceding year must pay either 90 percent of the current year's tax liability or 112 percent of the prior year's tax liability. The 112 percent figure will become 110 percent starting in 2003. Individuals with AGI not exceeding $150,000 must pay either 90 percent of the current tax year liability or 100 percent of the prior year's tax liability. These provisions allow individuals who cannot easily estimate their income before year-end to avoid penalties by basing estimated tax payments on the prior year's tax liability.

Estimated tax payments are generally made in four equal installments, on April 15, June 15, September 15, and January 15. However, if you don't receive income evenly throughout the year, you can make estimated tax payments based on actual income for the period. Be careful to pay the right amount with each installment—paying extra in later periods does not exempt you from penalties for underpayments in earlier periods.

TIP It is important to review your tax situation early in the year so you make proper estimated tax payments and avoid penalties.

Why You Don't Want a Tax Refund

Don't view your tax refund as a forced savings program. If you're concerned that you would just spend the difference each paycheck, you could have that amount automatically transferred to an investment account every pay period. (Remember that an automatic investing plan, such as dollar cost averaging, does not assure a profit or protect against a loss in declining markets.)

If too much federal tax is being withheld from your paycheck, fill out a new W-4 to determine how many allowances you should claim. Don't confuse allowances with the exemptions claimed on your tax return. You can claim additional allowances for items such as itemized deductions that exceed the standard deduction, child tax credits, and education credits.

Taxes and Your Investment Portfolio

Taxes are deducted from my paycheck, and I pay taxes on the things I buy with the paycheck. I know I must pay taxes on any early investment withdrawals. How do taxes affect my investment portfolio?

Pat D. of Indianapolis, IN

A major concern for many people is how they will be taxed on their investment portfolio. And it's easy to see why. After working so hard to earn and save money, we want to keep as much of it as we can. However, you don't want to be so concerned with avoiding or deferring taxes that you delay investing your money.

No matter what your tax strategy, the number one thing for everyone to do is to start saving now. Once you are saving consistently, we can talk about the best way to approach the tax aspects of investing.

You have many investment vehicles available to you today, some of which are offered on an after-tax basis. There are several advantages to an after-tax account, including no government restrictions on how much or when you can contribute and the ability to withdraw the principal amount without penalty or taxation.

Individual retirement accounts (IRAs) are another good way for many people to save. Although eligibility requirements for tax deductibility vary, traditional IRAs are generally a good way to defer taxes and accumulate funds. (Withdrawals are taxed as ordinary income and may be subject to a 10 percent federal penalty if made prior to age fifty-nine and a half.) The Roth IRA is also an attractive option for many people. While contributions to the Roth IRA are not tax deductible, qualified distributions of capital gains and earnings are federal-tax free.

FYI

While tax considerations do play a part in your investment portfolio, they should not be a determining factor. The best thing to do is start saving now and talk to a professional about creating a tax strategy for your portfolio. ■

(Qualified Roth IRA distributions may be subject to state and local taxes, depending upon your state.) In addition, qualified early withdrawals of contributions are permitted on a tax- and penalty-free basis. If you are investing in an IRA, pay attention to how your money is invested.

Think Taxes All Year!

Waiting until December to review tax strategies may mean that you won't have time to implement some valid tax-saving strategies. Be sure to consider the following three options:

1. *Review investment strategies.*

Those individuals with marginal tax rates of 31 percent, 36 percent, or 39.6 percent should keep in mind that the capital gains tax rate is 28 percent. Growth stocks and growth mutual funds may seem more attractive now, but don't venture into these investments unless they meet your specific goals and you are willing to hold them for the long term.

Municipal bonds are another investment that may appear attractive to higher-income taxpayers. Some investments allow you to postpone paying taxes on income earned until you withdraw those earnings, including annuities, whole life insurance policies, and nondeductible individual retirement accounts (IRAs).

2. *Shelter income.*

Contributions to a 401(k), Keogh, deductible IRA, and simplified employee pension (SEP) allow you to defer interest earnings as well as exclude the amount of your contribution from your taxable income. Many fringe benefits provided by employers are tax-free, so review all available benefits.

3. *Shift income.*

You can shift $11,000 ($22,000 with your spouse) per year to any number of individuals. Not only does this reduce your taxable estate, but you avoid paying taxes on any earnings on those assets.

Organize all of your tax records by:

- Gathering all the forms sent to you by third parties—W-2's, 1099's, K-1's, et cetera.
- Collecting receipts and canceled checks that document deductions you plan to take.
- Pulling together documentation for nonroutine transactions, such as the sale of securities.

New Tax Strategies

I know my mind is not as sharp as it used to be, but I seem to recall that some kind of tax law changed in 1996 that affected IRAs. Can you help shed some light on this mystery?

Bob F. of Laredo, TX

Based on changes made by the 1996 Small Business, Health Insurance, and Welfare Reform Acts signed into law in August 1996,* several new tax strategies are available that may help reduce your income taxes.

- The amount of a spousal individual retirement account (IRA) contribution was increased to $2,000, even if one of the spouses has less than $2,000 of compensation (or even no compensation). However, the combined contributions of the two spouses cannot exceed their combined compensation. The deductibility rules have not changed.
- Certain withdrawals can be made from IRAs before the age of fifty-nine and a half without paying the 10 percent early withdrawal penalty. Two exceptions are provided: (1) to pay medical expenses in excess of 7.5 percent of adjusted gross income and (2) to pay for medical insurance when a person has received unemployment compensation (if certain conditions are met).
- For amounts received in 1997, 1998, or 1999, the 15 percent

---

*Tax law changes in 2001 raised the $2,000 contribution to $3,000.

excess distribution tax is waived on qualified plan or IRA withdrawals in excess of $160,000 for annual distributions or $800,000 for lump-sum distributions (amounts indexed annually for inflation). Individuals may wish to consider accelerating some or all of their pension distributions.

- Beginning in 1997, employees who work past the age of seventy and a half can defer taking distributions from qualified plans until April 1 of the year following retirement. Withdrawals still must be made from IRAs by April 1 of the year following the year you turn seventy and a half.

- Five-year forward averaging of lump-sum distributions will be eliminated beginning in tax years after 1999. You may want to move your retirement date up if this will have a significant impact on your tax liability.

- Tax credits will be available for adoption expenses. A dollar-for-dollar tax credit is available for up to $5,000 per child of qualified adoption expenses incurred after 1996 ($6,000 for special needs children). The credit is phased out for taxpayers with adjusted gross income over certain levels. Employer-provided adoption assistance up to an additional $5,000 can be excluded from taxable income, subject to the phaseout provisions.

- Long-term-care insurance and expenses are now deductible on your tax return as a medical expense. Benefits from these policies will be excluded from taxable income, similar to medical insurance benefits.

Making Lifetime Gifts

Estate taxes have shifted over the years so much that I can no longer keep up. What's the latest?

Craig S. of Ft. Wayne, IN

Since estate taxes are scheduled to be phased out gradually and then reinstated in 2011, you may still want to make gifts during your lifetime to reduce your taxable estate. Some tips to consider include:

- Use your annual gift-tax exclusion amount. Every year you can make gifts up to $11,000 ($22,000 if the gift is split with your spouse) to any individual free of gift taxes. This amount is adjusted annually for inflation, in $1,000 increments. You can make these gifts to any number of individuals. Any future appreciation or income generated on these gifts is also removed from your estate.

- Pay medical and education expenses for your heirs. Certain amounts paid directly to institutions for these expenses can be made gift-tax free.

- Consider using your lifetime gift exclusion. This exclusion increased to $1 million in 2002 and is in addition to your annual gift-tax exclusion amount. Thus, those with estates large enough to be subject to estate taxes may consider using this exclusion to remove assets from their taxable estate.

- Look into ways to maximize the benefit of your exclusion amounts. For instance, individuals who transfer noncontrolling interests in businesses, farms, real estate, and other assets during their lifetime may be able to assign a minority interest discount to the gift's value. Gifting assets to certain types of trusts, such as qualified personal residence trusts and grantor retained annuity trusts, allows you to place an asset in trust now, use the asset for a period of time, and thus place a lower value on the gift.

- Eliminate making taxable gifts to heirs for now. The scheduled phaseout of the estate tax means that more estates will be able to minimize the payment of estate taxes.

- Gift property that has the potential to increase in value but has not already done so. A lifetime gift-tax basis remains your original basis plus any gift tax paid. Thus, if you gift an asset with a low basis, your heirs could owe significant capital gains tax when the asset is sold.

- Make charitable contributions during your lifetime. Charitable contributions made after death are free of estate taxes. With the future of the estate tax uncertain, you may want to make charitable contributions during your life. Those contributions still lower your taxable estate and will also allow you to receive an income tax deduction for the contributions.

■ Keep your own needs in mind. While gifting can be a valuable estate-planning strategy, you don't want to gift so much of your estate that you have difficulty making ends meet later in life.

The 18 Percent Capital Gains Tax Rate

I just got an apartment building in a divorce settlement. Even though I did not know about the building until I filed for divorce, I do know a little about capital gains tax. What is the rate these days?

Ernestine M. of Janesville, IA

For assets acquired after December 31, 2000, and held for more than five years, capital gains will be taxed at an 18 percent rate. (For taxpayers who ordinarily would be taxed at the 10 percent rate, the rate is 8 percent for assets held longer than five years, regardless of when they were acquired.)

Wondering why you should worry about this now, when you won't be able to take advantage of this rate until 2006? You can make a deemed-sale-and-repurchase election to treat readily tradable stock held on January 1 as if you sold it on January 2 for its closing market price and then repurchased it for the same price. Your tax basis is then increased or decreased to the stock's fair market value. You can make the same election for other capital assets, using their fair market value on January 2. Any gains resulting from this election must be recognized on your next tax return. Losses can't be recognized for tax purposes, but your tax basis is adjusted to reflect the loss. Making the election rather than actually selling the assets allows you to avoid any transaction costs. The election can be made any time during the year, giving you an opportunity to gauge your overall tax situation before making the election.

But does it make sense to recognize gain now to reduce your capital gains tax rate by 2 percent on assets you hold for five years? You may want to consider this strategy if you only have a small amount of gain on the asset and expect it to appreciate significantly during the next five years. Or, this strategy may make sense if you have capital losses that can be used to offset any gains.

Investment Tax Strategies

I think it is time for me to start rethinking my investment strategies. One of the key things I need to know is how to handle the payment of income taxes.

Ernest W. of Silver Spring, MD

The payment of income taxes on your investment income and gains can significantly reduce your total return. Thus, you should look for sound strategies to help you reduce the impact of taxes on your portfolio. Consider the following:

- Carefully decide which investments to hold in tax-advantaged and taxable accounts. Gains from investments held in retirement accounts, such as 401(k) plans and traditional individual retirement accounts (IRAs), are taxed at ordinary income tax rates when withdrawn, rather than the lower capital gains tax rates. While it may make sense to hold investments that produce ordinary income in retirement accounts and investments that produce capital gains in taxable accounts, factors such as your investment period should also be considered.
- Take advantage of tax-deferred or tax-exempt investments. Consider investing in municipal bonds, since their interest income in most cases is exempt from federal income taxes and possibly state income taxes. (There may be alternative minimum tax consequences and an impact on taxation of Social Security benefits.) Make contributions to your 401(k) plan and/or IRAs. The deferral of income taxes can make a significant difference in the ultimate size of your portfolio.

Tax Planning under the New Tax Act

With so many provisions of the Economic Growth and Tax Relief Reconciliation Act of 2001 (Tax Act) scheduled to phase in over a period of years, it can be difficult to determine how the new tax rules will affect your tax-planning strategies. Some strategies to consider based on the provisions of the Tax Act include:

- With tax rates decreasing over the next several years, pay particular attention to the timing of income and deductions. To the extent possible, deductions should be accelerated while rates are higher and income deferred until rates are lower. Some deductions that can be accelerated include payment of property taxes, estimated state taxes, medical expenses, and charitable contributions. Income that can typically be deferred includes self-employment income, year-end bonuses, and commissions.

- Consider shifting income to children over age fourteen to take advantage of the new 10 percent tax bracket.

- Since individual tax rates will eventually be lower than corporate rates, business owners who have business income taxed at a corporate level may want to reconsider their choice of corporate entity. Sole proprietorships, partnerships, S corporations, and limited liability corporations have income taxed at the individual level, thus taking advantage of lower rates and avoiding double taxation.

- Get ready to start contributing additional money to individual retirement accounts (IRAs) and qualified retirement plans, especially if you are age fifty or over. Limits on contributions start to increase in 2002, and individuals age fifty or over can start to make additional catch-up contributions. Even if you don't think you'll need the additional funds for retirement, recent changes in the minimum distribution rules make IRAs and qualified plans good vehicles for transferring assets to heirs.

- If you are funding children's education costs, take another look at education IRAs and qualified tuition programs.

Starting in 2002, both offer tax-free distributions for qualified education expenses, making them attractive ways to save for education expenses. The limit for contributions to education IRAs has increased from $500 to $2,000. Higher-income taxpayers may be especially interested in qualified tuition programs, since there are no income phase-outs for contributions and larger contributions can be made (up to $50,000 in one year that can be counted as annual $10,000 tax-free gifts for five years).

■ Don't make the mistake of thinking that you no longer have to plan your estate due to the eventual repeal of the estate tax. Future legislation can undo or significantly change the provisions in the Tax Act. Even if the estate tax is repealed in 2010, your estate plan should consider strategies to deal with estate taxes in the event you die before then. You probably don't want to undo any estate-planning strategies already in place, and you may want to consider strategies that won't result in the payment of gift taxes.

■ Continue an annual gifting program, since it won't result in the payment of any gift taxes. In addition, any future appreciation or income generated on those gifts is removed from your estate.

■ Consider using your lifetime gift exclusion during your lifetime. This increased to $1 million in 2002. This strategy does not result in the payment of any gift taxes and reduces your taxable estate in the event you die before 2010.

■ Keep turnover in your portfolio to a minimum. Purchase investments that you'll be comfortable owning for years. That way, you can let any unrealized capital gains grow for many years.

■ Analyze the tax consequences before rebalancing your portfolio. Portfolio rebalancing is a taxable event that may result in a taxable gain or loss. In general, avoid selling investments from

your taxable portfolio for reasons other than poor performance. Bring your asset allocation back in line through other
methods. For instance, when purchasing new investments,
select ones from underweighted categories. Or, rebalance
through your tax-deferred accounts, which generally won't
result in a current tax liability.

■ Consider donating appreciated stock held over one year to
charity. You will receive a charitable credit for the fair value of
the stock, and you avoid paying capital gains taxes on the gain.
The donation amount is subject to limitation, based on a percentage of your adjusted gross income.

■ Look at your holding period before selling. Keep in mind that
your gains on investments held for over a year are taxed at a
maximum capital gains tax rate of 20 percent (10 percent if
you're in the 15 percent marginal tax bracket), while gains on
investments held for less than a year are taxed at your ordinary
income tax rate. The capital gains tax rate of 20 percent is significantly lower than the maximum ordinary income tax rate
of 39.6 percent, so you may be able to save significant taxes by
timing your sales.

■ Consider selling investments with losses to offset gains. The
best tax strategy may be to recognize losses that completely
offset your capital gains and generate an additional $3,000
loss, since up to $3,000 of excess losses can be deducted
against ordinary income. If you believe the investment has the
potential to increase in value, you can deduct the loss and
repurchase it as long as you avoid the wash sale rules. These
rules state that you must repurchase the shares at least thirty-
one days after you sell the original investment to recognize the
loss for tax purposes.

■ Keep accurate records of your cost basis. For instance, rein-
vested dividends are part of your cost basis, since income
taxes were paid in the year the dividends were received. For
inherited assets, the cost basis is typically the value on the date
of the previous owner's death.

■ When selling only part of your investment, evaluate which portion to sell. In many cases, you'll want to sell the highest-cost shares first to reduce your gains. However, the holding period of those shares and your current-year income tax position should also be considered.

Chapter 6

Your Portfolio at a Glance

The Composition of the S&P 500

I consider myself a savvy investor who keeps abreast of market trends. I even started making online stock trades. The online company I use recently recommended a company that it said is at the top of the S&P 500 list. Now, what is the S&P 500 and why should I care?

Charmaine G. of Seattle, WA

The Standard & Poor's 500 (S&P 500) is an unmanaged index of five hundred large-company stocks generally considered representative of the U.S. stock market. It is a market-weighted index, meaning it factors in the differences in individual stock size by multiplying the price of each by the number of shares outstanding. Thus, larger companies have a greater influence on the index than smaller companies.

While investors cannot invest directly in an index, approximately $1 trillion is invested in index funds designed to track the performance of the S&P 500 (Source: Standard & Poor's Corporation, 2001). In addition, the returns of the S&P 500 are used by a tremendous number of individuals and mutual funds to benchmark their portfolio's performance.

Decisions regarding the removal and addition of companies to the S&P 500 are made by the Index Committee at Standard & Poor's Corporation. Companies cannot apply for inclusion in the index, and decisions are made based on public information.

Factors That Can Cause a Stock to Be Removed from the S&P 500

- *Merger and acquisition.* Mergers and acquisitions are reviewed to determine whether the remaining company should be removed or left in the index. Historically, this has been the most common reason for removal.
- *Bankruptcy.* A company is immediately removed from the index when bankruptcy is filed.
- *Restructuring.* A major restructuring is thoroughly analyzed to determine whether the company should remain in the index or be removed.
- *Lack of representation.* Companies can be removed from the index if they no longer meet current criteria for inclusion and/or they are no longer representative of their industry group. Factors that could lead to removal include a decline in market size, belonging to a declining industry, or illiquidity of the stock.

When a stock is removed from the S&P 500, it is replaced by a company meeting the following criteria:

- *Liquidity.* Liquidity is measured as average monthly trading volume divided by shares outstanding. That number must equal 0.3 for New York Stock Exchange and American Stock Exchange shares and 0.6 for Nasdaq shares. The Index Committee also looks at the stock's price history, attempting to minimize the number of single-digit-priced stocks in the index.
- *Ownership.* Sufficient shares must be available for investors to purchase. Two conditions must be met: no single entity can own more than 50 percent of the outstanding shares, and

multiple entities may not hold more than 60 percent of the outstanding shares.

- *Fundamental analysis.* The company must have at least four quarters of positive operating net income. However, occasionally, a company with a loss will be included if it would have been profitable except for a loss due to a merger or acquisition.
- *Market capitalization.* While there are no strict dollar values, the company must be a leading company in a leading U.S. industry. Generally, market capitalization is over $4 billion.
- *Sector representation.* The Index Committee attempts to keep each sector's weight in the index proportionate to that sector's weighting in the universe of stocks.

While changes to the S&P 500 used to be fairly rare, they have increased in recent years. For instance, between 1991 and 1993, there were five to twelve changes per year. From 1998 to 2000, however, there were between forty and sixty changes per year (Source: *Money,* July 2001).

These changes have had a significant impact on the S&P 500's composition. For instance, between December 1980 and July 2000, the number of technology stocks in the S&P 500 increased from eighteen to seventy-eight, increasing that sector's market capitalization from 8 percent to 35 percent of the index. However, the Index Committee maintains that the change was necessary for the S&P 500 to keep pace with the technology sector's increase in the overall stock market, from 13 percent to 40 percent of total capitalization (Source: *Standard & Poor's General Criteria for S&P 500 U.S. Index Membership,* September 2000).

The Art of Rebalancing

I have finally convinced my new wife to rethink some of her investments. It took her a long time to develop her portfolio, and I know if she loses money because of my advice, I'm out. Can you give us some tips?

Michael C. of Silver Spring, MD

Since different investments have varying rates of return, your asset allocation will stray from your desired allocation over time. Thus, you should periodically review your portfolio to see if it needs to be rebalanced. Some points to keep in mind include:

- Decide how much variation you are willing to tolerate in your portfolio. It is difficult to maintain your portfolio at precise percentages, so you may want to allow some leeway. For instance, you might monitor your portfolio more closely when an asset class varies by 5 percent and start to rebalance when it varies by 10 percent. But make sure you adhere to these guidelines. Sometimes it can be difficult to sell an asset that is performing well and reinvest those funds in assets that are not doing as well. However, your asset allocation strategy was designed to help manage the overall risk in your portfolio. By allowing one asset class to dominate, you increase your portfolio's risk.

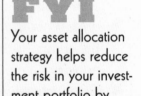

Your asset allocation strategy helps reduce the risk in your investment portfolio by determining what percentage of various asset classes to hold. ■

- Review your overall allocation strategy. Over time, your strategy may change as your financial goals and objectives change. For instance, you may want a high percentage of your portfolio in stocks when you are younger, but may want to shift more to fixed-income investments as you approach retirement age. However, don't use this review as an excuse to arbitrarily change your allocation. For instance, don't cut way back on your stock allocation simply because you're uncomfortable with the recent stock market movements.

- Evaluate the tax ramifications before selling assets from taxable accounts. If selling an asset for rebalancing purposes will result in a tax liability, look for other ways to accomplish this goal. For instance, you may be able to rebalance in your tax-deferred portfolio, which typically won't result in a tax liability. Or any new investments can be placed in assets that are underweighted in your portfolio. You can redirect periodic interest, dividends, and capital gains to other asset classes rather than reinvesting them in the same asset. Any withdrawals can be made from overweighted asset classes.

How Are You Handling Risk?

Typically, before deciding how much to allocate to different investment categories, you answer several questions about your tolerance for risk. The recent stock market fluctuations have provided a real-world test of your theoretical answers. You should now have a better understanding of your comfort level with risk, making this a good time to reassess your risk tolerance.

There are at least two components to your risk tolerance. One is the appropriate level of investment risk based on your personal situation. Factors such as your time horizon for investing, income level, total assets, debt levels, liquidity, and family responsibilities may affect that decision.

The other element is your emotional tolerance for risk. Even if your personal situation indicates a high level of risk, that may not be prudent if you don't feel emotionally comfortable with that risk. How you've handled the recent stock market fluctuations should provide a good indication of your emotional comfort level with risk. How have you reacted during this volatile period? Have you taken the fluctuations in stride, or have you been anxious about your portfolio's value? Have you frequently calculated your portfolio's value or only occasionally checked? Have you been tempted to sell all your stock investments, or did you realize that this is just a normal part of the investing process? What would you do if the market continued to decline? How long could you withstand a declining market before feeling compelled to sell?

TIP If you've had difficulty handling the recent market fluctuations, try to reduce your portfolio's risk to gain more comfort.

Dividends versus Stock Buyback Programs

Many years ago I purchased stock in the company that I worked for. Although they no longer employ me, I've kept the stock. Recently I got a notice in the mail that said that stockholders have the option of participating in a stock buyback program instead of receiving the usual dividends. What's the difference?

Myron G. of Miami, FL

With dividends, the company decides when investors receive distributions, which the investors must pay income taxes on at ordinary income tax rates. With a stock repurchase program, the company systematically repurchases shares in the open market and then either retires the stock or uses it for employee stock options. If the stock repurchase program results in higher stock prices, the shareholder doesn't pay taxes on any capital gains until the shares are sold. When the shares are sold, provided the stock has been held for at least one year, capital gains tax rates, rather than ordinary rates, will be paid on the gains.

When using excess cash to reward investors, companies have two main options—to pay cash dividends or to buy back shares of stock. ∎

How would a repurchase program increase a stock's price? A buyback program is often viewed as a signal that the company's management feels the stock is cheap relative to its business potential, which can increase interest in the stock. Also, if the shares are purchased and retired, earnings per share (EPS) will increase, since the number of shares used in the EPS calculation decreases. Each shareholder's percentage of the total stock owned also increases, since fewer shares are outstanding.

Dividend programs are viewed as long-term commitments, while stock buyback programs are considered one-time financial commitments. ∎

How does a company decide between dividends or a stock repurchase program? Typically, dividends are

STRATEGIES FOR REDUCING YOUR PORTFOLIO'S RISK

- Diversify your portfolio among several investment categories, including cash, bonds, and stocks, as well as within investment categories, such as owning several types of stocks. A properly diversified portfolio should contain a mix of asset types whose values have historically moved in different directions or in the same direction with different magnitudes. The theory is that when one asset class is declining, other assets may be increasing in value.

- Stay in the market through different market cycles. Remaining in the market over the long term helps to reduce the risk of receiving a lower return than expected, especially for more volatile investments, such as stocks.

- Become familiar with different investments and their risks. Over time, your comfort level with risk should increase as your understanding increases.

- Maintain reasonable return expectations. Otherwise, you may become disappointed if an asset does not perform as expected.

- Don't accumulate cash, waiting for a large sum to invest. Many investors feel it is less risky to invest smaller sums rather than one large amount.

- If you're not sure you can handle the risk associated with more aggressive investments, start out by investing a small amount. Increase your exposure as your comfort level increases.

paid by companies with permanent excess operating cash flows, while repurchase programs are used by companies with nonrecurring cash flows. Companies with nonrecurring cash flows do not want to pay dividends because they might have to reduce or eliminate them in the future, an action typically viewed harshly by the markets.

Reducing the Risks of Bond Investing

I would love to invest money in bonds. My father says only rich folks can withstand the risks. How do I avoid some of the risks?

Carmen G. of Washington, DC

Investments are affected by different types of risk. While you can't totally eliminate these risks, you can develop strategies to help you manage them. The risks associated with bonds include:

■ *Interest rate risk.*

Interest rates and bond prices move in opposite directions. A bond's price will rise in value when interest rates fall and decrease in value when interest rates rise. This occurs because the existing bond's price changes to provide the same return as an equivalent, newly issued bond at prevailing interest rates. The longer the bond's maturity, the greater the impact of interest rate changes. Also, the effects of interest rate changes on market value tend to be less significant for bonds with higher-coupon interest rates.

To help you manage this risk, consider holding the bond to maturity. This eliminates the impact of interest rate changes, since the total principal value will be paid at maturity. Thus, selecting a maturity date that coincides with your cash needs will help you manage interest rate risk. However, you may still receive an interest-income stream that is lower than current rates. Selecting shorter maturities or staggering the bond maturities can also help you with this risk.

■ *Reinvestment risk.*

You typically know what interest income you'll receive from a bond. But you must then take that periodic income and reinvest it, usually at varying interest rates. Your principal may also mature at a time when interest rates are low.

Staggering maturities over a period of time (laddering) can help you lessen reinvestment risk. Since the bonds in your ladder mature every year or so, you reinvest the principal over a period of time instead of in one lump sum.

■ *Inflation risk.*

Since bonds typically pay a fixed amount of interest and principal, the purchasing power of those payments decreases due to inflation, which is a major risk for intermediate- and long-term bonds.

Investing in short-term bonds reduces inflation's impact, since you are frequently reinvesting at prevailing interest rates. You can also consider inflation-indexed securities issued by the U.S. government, which pay a real rate of return above inflation.

■ *Default and credit risk.*

Default risk is the risk that the issuer will not be able to pay the interest and/or principal. Credit risk is the risk that the issuer's credit rating will be reduced, which will likely decrease the bond's value.

To help you reduce this risk, consider purchasing U.S. government bonds or bonds with investment-grade ratings. Continue to monitor the credit ratings of any bonds purchased.

■ *Call risk.*

Call provisions allow bond issuers to replace high-coupon bonds with lower-coupon bonds when interest rates decrease.

U.S. government securities do not have call provisions. However, most corporate and municipal bonds have call provisions. Review the call provisions before purchase to select those most favorable to you.

Keep in mind that the assumption of risk is generally rewarded with higher return. One of the safest bond strategies is to purchase only three-month Treasury bills, but this typically results in the lowest return. To increase your return, you should decide which risks you are comfortable assuming and devise a corresponding bond strategy.

Put Time on Your Side

Eight days ago, I invested money in the market, and I have watched it every day since. Nothing has happened. Why? Should I change my strategy?

Diane R. of Las Vegas, NV

The Advantages of Asset Allocation

Your asset allocation strategy represents your personal decisions about how much of your portfolio to allocate to various investment categories, such as stocks, bonds, cash, and other alternatives. When stock market returns were above average for an extended period, investors did not have much interest in asset allocation. Then, the best strategy seemed to be to own only stocks. But with the recent stock market declines, investors are again looking at asset allocation. Some of the advantages of an asset allocation strategy include:

- Providing a disciplined approach to diversification. An asset allocation strategy is another name for diversification, an important strategy for reducing portfolio risk.

- Encouraging long-term investing. An asset allocation strategy is designed to control your portfolio's long-term makeup. It should not change based on economic conditions or market fluctuations.

- Reducing the risk in your portfolio. Investments with higher returns typically have higher risk and more volatility in year-to-year returns. Asset allocation combines more aggressive investments with less aggressive ones. This combination can help reduce your portfolio's overall risk.

- Adjusting your portfolio's risk over time. Your portfolio's risk can be adjusted by changing allocations for the different investments you hold. By anticipating changes in your personal situation, you can make these portfolio changes gradually.

- Focusing on the big picture. Staying focused on your asset allocation strategy will help prevent you from investing in assets that won't help accomplish your goals. It gives you a framework for making reasoned investment decisions rather than investing in a haphazard manner.

You may think you should watch your investments on a daily basis, keeping track of every fluctuation. Yet, you're probably investing for long-term goals that may take decades to achieve. Your long-term success will be more dependent on how well you implement four fundamental principles:

1. Invest as soon as possible.

Compounding of earnings can have a dramatic impact on the ultimate size of your portfolio. Consider the following example. Four individuals, age twenty, thirty, forty, and fifty, each invest $5,000 this year. What will that balance equal when each individual reaches age sixty-five, assuming an 8 percent rate of return compounded annually? The following table summarizes the results:*

	Years Invested	Ending Balance
50-year-old	15	$ 15,861
40-year-old	25	34,242
30-year-old	35	73,927
20-year-old	45	159,602

Even though everyone invested the same amount, the twenty-year-old has a much larger balance due to compounding of earnings.

2. Invest regularly.

Don't make the mistake of not starting an investment program because you don't think you have enough to start investing. Over a period of time, even a modest investment program can grow significantly. Assume you start investing $2,000 a year when you are age thirty and earn 8 percent compounded annually. The balance would grow to the following amounts:

---

*The tables and examples in this chapter are provided for illustrative purposes only and are not intended to project the performance of a specific investment. They do not take into account the effects of commissions or any taxes that may be due.

After 1 year	$ 2,160
After 5 years	12,672
After 10 years	31,291
After 20 years	98,846
After 35 years	372,204*

*Keep in mind that an automatic investing plan, such as dollar cost averaging, does not assure a profit or protect against loss in declining markets. Because such a program involves periodic investment, consider your financial ability and willingness to continue purchases through periods of low price levels.

3. Invest more.

Even modest changes in the amount you invest can dramatically increase your portfolio's value. Consider the example of a thirty-five-year-old man who is debating whether to make annual investments of 6 percent ($3,000) or 8 percent ($4,000) of his $50,000 salary. If he earns 8 percent compounded annually, his investments at age sixty-five would equal $339,850 with 6 percent contributions and $453,133 with 8 percent contributions. Each increase of 2 percent ($1,000) of his pay would require additional investments of $30,000 over thirty years, but would increase his ending balance by $113,283.

4. Invest in appropriate investments.

Although you shouldn't invest based solely on anticipated returns, even modest changes in your return can have a substantial impact on the ultimate size of your investments. The following table shows the ultimate value of $1, based on various rates of return and years invested.

> **TIP** When assembling your portfolio, you should not only assess the targeted risk-and-return characteristics of an individual investment but should also consider the impact that investment will have on your total portfolio.

Rate of Return	Years			
	10	20	30	40
3%	1.34	1.81	2.43	3.26
4%	1.48	2.19	3.24	4.80
5%	1.63	2.65	4.32	7.04
6%	1.79	3.21	5.74	10.29
7%	1.97	3.87	7.61	14.97
8%	2.16	4.66	10.06	21.72
9%	2.37	5.60	13.27	31.41
10%	2.59	6.73	17.45	45.26
11%	2.84	8.06	22.89	65.00
12%	3.11	9.65	29.96	93.05

Taking Stock

My wife has been bugging me for years to purchase stock. Last month I did. Well, now she has started telling me that I need to monitor my investment. I thought all you needed to do was to buy the stuff.

George S. of St. Louis, MO

Your work isn't finished once you've selected stocks for your portfolio. Even if you are a buy-and-hold investor, you should monitor your stocks on an ongoing basis to ensure they continue to meet your investment objectives. Consider monitoring the following:

- *Stock prices.* On a weekly or monthly basis, track the prices of your individual stocks. Share prices typically react quickly to changes in the market's view about a company's future, so rapid price changes can alert you to major changes at a company. You can then look for news announcements that may explain the sudden price change.

- *Quarterly earnings reports and dividend distributions.* Read quarterly earnings reports, paying particular attention to whether earnings are in line with expectations. Make sure any dividends are for expected amounts, finding out why large unexpected increases or decreases occurred.

- *Annual reports.* Read the annual report carefully for explanations about the company's financial performance and operations. While the wealth of information can seem overwhelming, reviewing key information can provide insights into a company's operations and prospects for the future.

- *Stock performance compared to market performance.* At least annually, compare each stock's performance to a relevant benchmark. If the stock's performance is significantly lower than the overall market's performance, you may want to take a closer look to determine the reason.

- *Overall stock portfolio performance.* Reexamine your individual holdings annually to ensure that they still remain sound alternatives for your portfolio. Comparing your overall stock portfolio performance to a relevant benchmark will give you an indication of how well your investment approach is working.

Laddering Your Bond Portfolio

Three years ago, my mother starting giving bonds to each of her grandchildren as birthday gifts. I keep trying to figure out the best way to manage these bonds so that they can pay a portion of my daughter's tuition. But interest rates and maturity dates keep changing. How can I do this?

Bradley W. of Markham, IL

Uncertainty about the future direction of interest rates can make it difficult to decide on a bond maturity. This is a major concern, since interest rate changes can significantly affect the value of bonds, with the impact increasing as maturities lengthen. One strategy to handle this concern is to ladder your bonds over a series of maturity dates.

A bond ladder is a portfolio of bonds of similar amounts and types, maturing at different dates. For instance, a $30,000 portfolio might consist of six bonds of $5,000 each, maturing in six consecutive years. Since one bond matures every year or so, you reinvest the principal over a period of time rather than in one lump sum. If interest rates rise, you have money coming due every year or so to reinvest at the higher rates. In a declining interest rate environment, you will have some funds invested in longer-term bonds with higher interest rates and can reinvest maturing principal in other investments.

Laddering can also be used to help assure that money is available for a specific financial goal at a specific date. For instance, a bond ladder might mature in each of four consecutive years while a child is in college.

Your Stock Investing Strategy

My best friend watches way too much television. Every time she sees those ads for the investment firm that talks about how it selected a particular company, she goes out and buys stock in that company. Her portfolio looks like a checkerboard. What advice can you give her?

LaTica J. of Worcester, MA

She shouldn't make the mistake of just picking up stocks over the years without a stock selection methodology. Stock investment decisions can be made easier by approaching stocks in a systematic manner.

- Identify your investment goals. Before selecting individual stocks, you should decide what role stocks will have in your total portfolio. Make sure to answer these questions:

    Are you investing for the long or short term?

    How much money are you going to invest?

    Are you looking for income, capital appreciation, or a combination of the two?

How much risk are you willing to assume?

What rate of return are you targeting for your stock investments?

■ Decide which types of stocks are appropriate for your situation. Common stocks can be classified in many categories, including:

Blue chip. Stock of a major, well-established company with a history of earnings growth and dividend payments in both good and bad economic times.

Growth. Stock of a company whose sales and earnings are growing faster than the general economy and most other stocks. These companies typically invest their earnings back in the company to generate further growth, paying little in dividends.

Income. Stock of a company that pays stable, and often significant, dividends, providing investors with a steady stream of income.

Defensive. Stock of a company that is considered stable and comparatively safe in recessionary times, including utilities, banks, and food companies.

Cyclical. Stock of a company whose earnings tend to fluctuate sharply with the business cycle, such as auto companies.

Speculative. Stock of a company that is perceived to have more risk than other types of stocks, frequently including new stock issues and stocks in "hot" industries.

■ Decide on an overall stock investing strategy. Your strategy will help determine the types of stocks appropriate for your situation as well as how much time you'll need to devote to the investment process. A buy-and-hold strategy involves selecting a core group of stocks to be held for the long term. A stock timing strategy requires changes in your stock investments when market conditions change. Broad diversification involves investing in stocks from a variety of industries. Some investors prefer investing in one industry that may outperform the market, while others look for stocks that may increase substantially in a short time.

■ Analyze individual stocks. Research individual stocks that may fit your overall strategy. While the wealth of information available about individual stocks can seem overwhelming, take time to evaluate annual reports, research reports, and other pertinent information.

Reevaluating Your Portfolio

Although I have investments, my plan was to wait for a couple of years before I touched them. I need to find out the best way of increasing my value, even in this economy.

Faith W. of Camden, NC

With the recent market declines, it may be painful to reevaluate your portfolio in depth, especially if your portfolio contains large losses. But this review is necessary to see if changes are needed to your portfolio. Some actions to consider include:

■ Review your investment objectives and determine whether your portfolio is helping you achieve those objectives. The purpose of investing is to help you achieve your financial goals—whether that is retirement, college funding, saving for a home, or some other financial need. First, determine whether your initial investment objectives are still valid or need to be changed. Then, decide whether your portfolio's performance is on track to helping you achieve those goals. Don't let the recent market declines cause you to abandon your overall investment strategy. With a long time horizon for investing, you should have time to overcome the recent market declines.

■ Measure your portfolio's performance against an appropriate benchmark. Look at every investment you own and factor in all costs when computing your return, including commissions, fees, and taxes. Once you've calculated your return for each investment, compare those returns to relevant benchmarks. A wide variety of indexes now exist, so find ones that track investments similar to each of your portfolio's components. This review should help put any declines in your portfolio into perspective and help identify parts of your portfolio that may need to be changed.

- Compare your portfolio's overall return to your estimated return. When designing your investment program, you assumed a rate of return that determined how much you needed to invest annually to help achieve your financial goals. Calculating your actual rate of return will help you ensure that you are on track to achieving your goals. If your actual return is significantly below what you estimated, you may have to increase the amount you are saving, invest in more aggressive alternatives, invest for a longer period, or decide you can settle for less money in the future.

- Review your portfolio's overall allocation, comparing it to your desired allocation. You may need to make changes for a variety of reasons. Assets that have performed well may now make up a larger percentage of your portfolio than planned. Or your asset allocation strategy may need refinement because of changing financial goals. For instance, as you approach retirement, you may want to shift part of your portfolio from stocks to bonds. However, don't make changes due simply to emotional factors or concerns about the market's recent declines.

Tips for Your Bond Holdings

I've got a new husband, three new stepkids, and a questionable investment portfolio. Honestly, I think his late wife set everything up before she died ten years ago. I need to carefully review everything, but before I make any changes I need help.

StaLinda W. of Pine Bluff, AR

Determine your objectives before investing. Decide how much of your portfolio you want invested in fixed-income securities.

■ Diversify your bond holdings among different bond types. Consider government, corporate, and municipal bonds, as well as different industries, credit ratings, and maturities.

■ Choose maturity dates for bonds carefully. When you need your principal is a major factor, but the current interest rate environment may also affect your decision.

■ Follow interest rate trends. At a minimum, follow the prime rate, Treasury bill rate, and Treasury bond rate. Understand the significance of the yield curve, and track its pattern over time.

■ Compare interest rates for specific bonds before investing. Interest rates can vary substantially between different bond types and between bonds with different maturities or credit ratings.

■ Research a bond before purchase. Review the credit quality, coupon rate, call provisions, and other significant factors. Determine whether the bond is appropriate for you in terms of risk, return, and maturity date.

■ Consider the tax aspects of the bond. By comparing the after-tax rate of return for various bonds, you may be able to increase your return. Depending on the bond, the interest income may be fully taxable or exempt from federal and/or state income taxes.

■ Review your bond holdings periodically. Evaluate the credit ratings of all your bonds at least annually to ensure that the ratings haven't been downgraded. Also, ensure that your holdings are still consistent with your overall investment objectives and asset allocation plan.

Chapter 7

Investment Strategies That Work

Investment Tune-ups

Twelve years ago, when I started my current job, I enrolled in a 401(k) account that included a mixed investment strategy. I don't know a lot about investments, and the agent who helped me pick out the plan no longer works for the company. This was a good plan; should I change it?

Nellie S. of Indianapolis, IN

The stock market is up and then the stock market is down. Now that a lot of African Americans have mutual funds in their 401(k) plans, they seem to think everything is all right. Investing for your future is a lot like maintaining a car for maximum mileage. As a car requires regular oil changes and tune-ups, your portfolio needs regular maintenance as well.

A long-term investment strategy does not imply a passive approach. Once your asset allocation is set, you should periodically review it. Your portfolio will need rebalancing over time because:

- Your investment objectives or personal circumstances can change. A change in your household's income may lead to an adjustment in the amount you earmark for investing. If you receive a raise or bonus, you might consider implementing a more aggressive asset allocation approach, or, if you retire or leave your job, you might have less income to invest. Family circumstances can also change; the birth of a child, for example, might encourage you to consider a long-term educational savings program, something that may not currently be included in your asset allocation.

- Your investments may grow at variable rates, changing the balance of the asset allocation. As the economy moves through its cycles, some investments will perform better than others. As this occurs, your asset allocation may be affected in different ways. If your stock holdings rise above your original allocation, your risk exposure increases, and if your stock holdings fall below their target, their growth potential may be lower.

Over time, the very nature of the market can throw your allocation out of balance. A regular review of the current state of your asset allocation will allow you to reassess the strategy required to help you achieve your long-term goals.

An Investment Road Map

My annual salary is only $40,000, but I have managed to invest $50 per month for the past four years. I get quarterly reports on how much my money earns, but it seems that my investments are not earning money as quickly as I would like.

Brian H. of Pittsburgh, PA

Every African American investor has unique needs and goals for the investment of his or her money. How, then, does an investor know how to measure success or failure? The answer to this question will differ from investor to investor, but here are a few common steps that can be taken to help assure that you do not stray too far from your goals:

- Define clear and measurable objectives. Without clearly defined goals, it is difficult to assess the success or failure of your investment program. Have you established these goals or has your investment allocation been merely reactionary? Try putting your goals in writing and checking back from time to time to help ensure that they still fit your needs.

- Strategize your asset allocation. Every investor would like the most return with the least risk. A unique investment policy means selecting the asset class that will help you meet this goal most efficiently. Each asset class and management style has its own unique volatility level, which correlates differently with other asset classes. Properly assembled, their collective attributes are designed to help your portfolio achieve maximum return with minimum risk.

Who Should Manage Your Investments?

My wife and I are both retired educators. Since we had only one child, we were able to save and invest enough money to live comfortably. Now that she has free time, my wife believes her background in education entitles her to take over management of our investments. Last month, she managed to lose money by switching from a slow but sure stock to a hot stock that was rising but then recently crashed. She is not qualified to handle our money.

Dennis B. of Galveston, TX

Managing your investments is not an easy task—you need to develop an investment strategy, evaluate numerous investment vehicles, and then monitor your investments on an ongoing basis. For those with a good grasp of investment basics, it is a time-consuming task that can seem overwhelming even if you are retired and have all day to work on it. And for those who struggle with investment concepts, the process can seem like an endless maze of choices.

Some reasons to consider an investment manager include:

- Investment managers actively control your portfolio, relieving you of much of the work.

- Some investors feel more comfortable when investment decisions are made by a full-time professional who spends most of his or her time analyzing the investment world.
- Although you won't be consulted on day-to-day decisions, you set the broad parameters that the manager uses, including specifications for asset allocation percentages.
- Managers will provide you with periodic performance statements, detailing investment returns.

> **TIP** Once your investment portfolio reaches the $50,000 to $100,000 level, you may want to consider using an investment manager to manage your investments.

If you're interested in hiring an investment manager, consider the following three steps:

1. Define your investment objectives.

Before deciding who should manage your investments, you should clearly state your investment objectives. Focus on your financial goals, time horizon for investing, return targets, income requirements, risk tolerance, and any personal restrictions you want to impose on investments.

2. Select a few possible investment managers.

At this point, you want to narrow the list down from the thousands of possible choices to a few compatible with your objectives. Financial professionals often monitor hundreds of different investment managers, maintaining information on investment styles, performance figures, personnel changes, methods for selecting investments, and many other factors.

3. Carefully evaluate those investment managers.

Consider asking the following questions:

- What are the firm's history and the principals' backgrounds? This will help you get an understanding of the firm's experience.
- What are the firm's investment philosophy and investment style? You want to ensure that the firm's philosophy and style are compatible with yours.

■ What are the minimum and maximum account sizes accepted? Also find out the total amount of assets under management and the number of clients serviced. This should give you an indication of how much personal attention you are likely to receive.

■ How are fees generated? You should be comfortable with the fee structure.

■ How is the firm's investment performance? Performance figures can be reported many different ways over varying time periods. Sometimes simply changing the reporting period by a month or two can produce much different results. If possible, obtain performance figures for the same time period for all managers you are evaluating. Keep in mind that past performance is not a guarantee of future results.

■ Can the firm provide you with client references? Current clients can provide you with valuable information.

When thinking about your investments and wondering what you should do, remember to be an individual. Stick to your investment plan for the long term and resist the commotion around you.

Important Home-Buying Decisions

I am a single woman who has been thinking of purchasing a home for a long time. What are some of the things I should consider before beginning my search?

Cheryl G. of Blue Island, IL

Buying a home has long been part of the American dream. But before you get caught up in the excitement of looking for your dream house, there are some important financial decisions that should be made. Those decisions include:

- How much should you spend on a house? An often-cited guideline indicates that your mortgage payment, insurance, and property taxes should not exceed 28 percent of your gross income. Nowadays, however, you can find lenders that let you spend up to 40 percent of your gross income on a mortgage payment. Rather than allowing your lender to dictate how much house you can afford, it's a better strategy to review your expenses, deciding how much you're comfortable devoting to a mortgage payment. You want to make sure that you'll still have money left over to put toward other financial goals and that unforeseen problems won't affect your ability to make your mortgage payment.

- How much do you have available for a down payment? Down payments on houses typically range from 5 percent to 20 percent of the total purchase price. Lower down payments make it easier to purchase a home, but they also increase the size of your mortgage and your mortgage payment. The ideal down payment is 20 percent of the total purchase price. With that large a down payment, you don't have to obtain private mortgage insurance, which typically runs from .25 percent to 1.25 percent of your total mortgage amount.

- What type of mortgage should you obtain? The two main types of mortgages are fixed-rate mortgages and adjustable-rate mortgages (ARMs). Fixed-rate mortgages are typically good choices for homeowners who plan on staying in their homes for many years. The fixed rate results in a fixed mortgage payment, making it easier to budget for other expenses. ARMs generally offer lower initial rates than fixed-rate mortgages, with the interest rate changing periodically based on a designated index. ARMs are often preferred by homeowners with rising incomes, those planning to move in a short time, and those who want the short-term cash flow benefits of lower interest rates.

- What mortgage term should you select? The most common terms are fifteen and thirty years. Thirty-year mortgages have lower monthly payments, but your equity builds slowly during the early years. Monthly payments for fifteen-year mortgages are typically 15 percent to 25 percent higher than 30-year mortgages, but the mortgage is paid off so much quicker that the total interest costs are less than half. Interest rates on fifteen-year loans are also generally lower than on thirty-year loans.

Before you get caught up in the excitement of finding your dream home, take time to work through these important home-buying decisions.

What's Your Investor Profile?

For the past year I have been trying to invest money. First I tried stocks, then I tried mutual funds, then my friend told me about IRAs. I'm confused. I don't know what type of investments would be best for me.

Lynette M. of New York, NY

Your investment strategy, including your asset allocation preferences, will give you a disciplined approach to making investment decisions. Before developing an investment strategy, however, you should answer some fundamental questions that will define your investor profile. Those questions include:

- What are your overall investment objectives? Investors committed to growth are looking for appreciation of capital, with little concern for income from their portfolio. Total return investors want a balance of income and capital appreciation. Income investors are looking for interest and dividend income, with capital appreciation a secondary concern. Individuals concerned about preservation of capital are most concerned with protecting their principal.

- What is your investment time frame? Short-term investors need their money in a year or two, while intermediate-term investors are investing for two to five years. A long-term investor is investing for at least five years. Typically, stock investments should only be considered by long-term investors. Because stock returns can be volatile, it is important to invest through different market cycles to reduce the chances that you will receive a lower return than expected.

- What is your risk tolerance? You should accurately gauge your tolerance for risk. If you take on too much risk, you may be tempted to sell an investment after a market downturn. Those uncomfortable with losing more than 5 percent of their principal in a year have a low risk tolerance and should consider short-term cash investments. A person with a moderate tolerance could stand a loss of 6 percent to 15 percent and should consider bonds and high-quality stocks. A person with a high risk tolerance could withstand a 16 percent to 25 percent loss and should consider more aggressive investments, such as growth stocks.

- What rate of return do you expect on your investments? Although past performance is not a guarantee of future results, reviewing historical rates of return for various investments can provide a rough estimate of potential returns. More aggressive investments usually have higher return potential.

- Are you concerned with reducing income taxes? Investors in higher tax brackets will want to consider investments that can help reduce income taxes. That might include municipal bonds, investments generating capital gains, and tax-deferred investments, such as 401(k) plans and individual retirement accounts (IRAs). Various investment strategies can also reduce the taxes you pay, such as holding capital gains investments for the long term.

> Your diversification decisions should help protect your portfolio during market downturns and help to reduce your portfolio's volatility.

Your Children and Investing

Investing is a topic that is not always taught in our school system. Thus, you may want to help teach your children investment basics by using some of these suggestions:

- Start discussing investment concepts at a young age. Look for opportunities to discuss investing concepts. You can explain the concept of compound interest when your bank statement arrives. Shopping trips can lead to discussions about how businesses operate and how individuals invest in those businesses. Help your child investigate which company manufactures a favorite toy or game. News reports about the closing prices of major stock indexes can lead to an explanation of how those indexes are calculated and what they measure. Newspapers can be used to show and explain stock quotes. While your children may not understand all these concepts at first, continued discussion increases their exposure to and familiarity with these concepts.

- Take advantage of field trips. Check if your local bank will give your children a brief tour. Some manufacturing companies offer tours, giving children an opportunity to see how companies operate. If you live in or visit New York, take your children to the New York Stock Exchange or the Federal Reserve. Visit the Bureau of Engraving and Printing in Washington, D.C. These tours can help make abstract concepts more concrete for your children.

- Explore investment Web sites devoted to children. Several excellent Web sites review investment basics in terms children understand. Go through some of them with your children, helping to reinforce some of the concepts presented.

- Explain your investment choices in your child's education fund. Discuss why you invested as you did, reviewing how well those investments have performed.

- Encourage your children to participate in stock simulation games. Several Web sites offer stock simulation games for children. Or you can set up a paper stock market simulation game at home. Participating in the game gives your children the opportunity to make investment choices and to learn more advanced topics as they progress through the game.

- Help your children purchase stocks. While stock simulation games can teach valuable lessons, your children are likely to take the whole subject more seriously when real money is involved. Minors cannot own stocks, so you will have to purchase the stock as custodian for your children. Let your children select the stocks, but make sure they research the stock first. Show them how to follow stock prices and how to review annual reports. Allow them to decide when to buy and sell, but first explain how transaction costs and taxes will reduce their return.

Watching the Economy When Investing

I just got my income tax refund. Before my boyfriend finds out how much money I got back, I need to start an investment plan. He thinks that the economy is too unstable. What difference does it make?

LaDenise T. of Charleston, SC

Since the economy can affect the stock and bond markets, investors who actively buy and sell are obviously concerned about it. But even investors who buy and hold their investments will probably want to keep an eye on the economy; thus, learning to read the signals sent by the economy can be important to all investors.

The state of the economy can affect many investment decisions:

- When to invest a large sum in the market
- Whether to invest new money in stocks or bonds
- When to sell investments to cover significant needs such as college expenses or retirement

Short-term trends in the stock and bond markets often seem random. By looking at longer time periods, one can see trends emerge that are often dependent on the overall economy. For investors, it may be even more important to look for signs that those trends are changing direction. With so much economic data available, how do you determine which indicators to watch? Three key statistics affect stocks and bonds:

1. *Interest rates.* Since bonds typically pay a fixed interest rate, changes in interest rates will affect the prices of existing bonds. Falling interest rates are good for bonds, since they increase the value of existing bonds. Interest rates are also important to stocks. Falling interest rates result in lower interest costs for both consumers and businesses. Consumers then tend to increase their purchases, helping to keep the economy strong. Increased spending and reduced interest costs help corporate profits go up, ultimately helping stock prices.

2. *Inflation.* Bondholders typically are interested in their real return, or their return after the effects of inflation. Interest rates tend to increase when inflation increases, since bondholders expect higher returns to compensate for the higher inflation.

3. *Corporate profits.* In an environment in which corporate profits are rising, stock prices tend to rise as well. When corporate earnings are falling, stock prices also tend to fall. Future earnings expectations can have a major impact on stock prices.

The trend in these three statistics will depend in large part on the economy's stage in the business cycle:

- As a recession starts, interest rates are poised to decrease, corporate profits are falling, and inflation is either stable or rising. Typically, stock prices may fall because of disappointing earnings and bonds may rally in anticipation of falling interest rates.
- Toward the end of a recession, interest rates, corporate profits, and inflation are all falling. Yet stock prices may start to rise as investors anticipate an economic recovery.

- During the early stages of an expansion, interest rates are still falling, corporate profits start to rise, and inflation continues to decline. Stock prices typically rise quickly during this time.
- As the expansion ages, interest rates start to rise and corporate profits continue to increase, but there are now concerns about inflation. Stocks may continue to do well until fears of a downturn set in. At this stage, you need to keep a close eye on the economy, since a recession may develop, which can rapidly bring stock prices down. Typically, you would not want to buy long-term bonds during this phase, since rising interest rates and the potential for rising inflation could decrease the bonds' value.

How do you tell if the economy is expanding? Generally, an expanding economy will have:

- Declining unemployment
- Increases in new jobs
- Rising industrial production
- Strong retail sales
- Strong auto sales
- Upbeat expectations from consumers

At times, these statistics can give conflicting signals, as can economists and other market commentators. In looking for guidance, you may want to review the Federal Reserve's (the Fed's) position. At each Federal Open Market Committee meeting, the previous meeting's minutes are published. Although those minutes may be a couple months old, the Fed indicates where it thinks the economy is headed, whether it is concerned about inflation or recession, and what actions it might take in the future. If you're interested, you'll find those minutes on the Fed's Web site at www.federalreserve.org.

Utilizing a Dollar Cost Averaging Strategy

The company where I worked since high school just went out of business. When I calculated all of my benefits, stock options, etc., I found that I should receive about $30,000. I want to invest it, but not all at once because I am afraid that I will lose my life savings. I heard something about dollar cost averaging. What is it?

Sadie H. of Gary, IN

One of the more difficult aspects of implementing an investment strategy is deciding when to invest. Fear of investing at a market high can keep investors waiting on the sidelines for some indication that it is a good time to invest. Unfortunately, the market never sends those messages.

Adopting a systematic investment approach takes away the need to make timing decisions. Once the plan is in place, you just follow it and continue investing on a periodic basis. The most common systematic investing approach is dollar cost averaging.

Dollar cost averaging involves investing a certain sum of money in the same investment on a periodic basis. For instance, instead of investing $48,000 in a particular stock immediately, you may decide to purchase $4,000 worth at the beginning of each of the next twelve months.

Since you invest a fixed amount of money each time, you purchase more shares when prices are lower and fewer shares when prices are higher. The average cost per share using dollar cost averaging is usually lower than the average market price per share over a given time period. However, if your investment increases in value over the investment period, you will pay more than by purchasing it all on the first day.

You may already use a dollar cost averaging program without realizing it. Participating in a 401(k) plan, reinvesting dividends in additional shares, and automatically transferring funds from a checking account to an investment account are all forms of dollar cost averaging.

Dollar cost averaging requires the discipline to invest consistently, regardless of market fluctuations. It is a good strategy for developing the habit of regularly setting aside money for investment. However, it does not ensure a profit or protect against losses. Before implementing a dollar cost averaging strategy, you should consider your financial ability to continue purchases through periods of high price levels.

Dollar cost averaging is a defensive strategy that can help protect you from making a major investment when prices are at a high, especially during volatile markets. This strategy may be well suited for investors who have uniform amounts of money to invest on a periodic basis, who follow a buy-and-hold strategy, or who do not want to attempt to forecast market movements.

Chapter 8

Funding a College Education

A Look at College Savings Programs

After ten years of marriage, my husband has filed for divorce. He says that in addition to child support, he will pay for our two sons' college education. I don't want to wait until they are in high school to start a college savings plan. I need information now so that the college savings plan can become part of our divorce decree.

Deana R. of Charlotte, NC

Qualified state tuition programs now come in two forms—prepaid tuition programs and college savings plans.

With prepaid tuition plans, you pay a fixed amount and are guaranteed sufficient funds to cover tuition at your state's public colleges or universities. Many plans also allow you to transfer a similar amount to a private or out-of-state university. Typically, you must be a resident of the state to enroll in the program.

With college savings plans, your money is invested in stocks, bonds, or mutual funds, with no guarantee as to how much will be available when your child enters college. Therefore, before investing, you should carefully review the plan's investment strategy, including investment choices and asset allocation policies. When your child enters college, funds can be withdrawn to pay any higher-education expenses, including tuition, fees, books, and room and board at any college or university. Some state programs accept only residents of that state, while other states will accept anyone.

A Helping Hand

When it comes to funding a child's college education, most parents need a helping hand. With all the forms to fill out, scholarships to apply for, and loans to research, it can be difficult to figure out how to secure the best overall financial aid package. Common mistakes often made during this process are:

- Assuming you are not eligible for financial aid
- Failing to file forms before the deadlines
- Not allowing enough time to complete all required paperwork
- Expecting the college to help you get financial assistance

All of these mistakes are avoidable—if you have someone working with you who understands the financial aid process.

If you are confused about the financial aid process, talk to a financial consultant who can:

- Help you select colleges that offer a good education with opportunities for financial assistance
- Review your financial aid documents to make sure they are accurate and that you are applying for all of the federal assistance programs for which you are eligible
- Negotiate with specific schools for a financial assistance package

Six Suggestions for Cutting College Costs

I am a high school junior who is being raised by a single mom. My mom works hard to support my four siblings and me. All of my life I have wanted to be a lawyer so that I can help underprivileged people who are taken advantage of because of their ignorance of the system. My mom cannot afford to pay for my tuition, so I need to do research to take care of it myself. Where do I start?

Kennetta J. of Austin, TX

As college costs continue to rise, the prospect of paying for four years of higher education can seem overwhelming. However, careful planning and thought can help reduce the total cost:

- Look at all types of scholarships. Many scholarships are not based on need. For example, academic, athletic, and music scholarships are often available to students who excel in those areas.

- Apply to several different colleges. Aid packages can vary significantly from school to school. This makes it wise to apply to several different schools, even if you prefer a particular college.

- Consider state public universities. State universities are partially funded by the state's taxpayers, so the costs for a public university in your state may be much more affordable than private universities.

- Negotiate with the university. If you are not satisfied with the aid package a school offers, talk to the university. Explaining your circumstances or showing the university an offer received from a different school may increase the financial aid package offered by that university.

- Start at a community college. Two-year colleges often are much cheaper than four-year colleges, especially since most students live at home while attending. First, however, determine which four-year college you will transfer to and make sure that all credits from the community college would transfer to the four-year college.

- Think about accelerating your studies. By taking spring and/or summer classes or extra credits throughout the year, it is possible to finish a four-year degree in three years—which saves a considerable amount of money.

Take Another Look at Education Savings Accounts

My parents started a college education fund for me when I was little. Next year I will receive my B.A. degree. My girlfriend just got pregnant and we want to start a college fund for our baby ASAP. Since I know we will not get married, this is the least I can do. Tell me how.

Stacy R. of Champaign-Urbana, IL

The Economic Growth and Tax Relief Reconciliation Act of 2001 (Tax Act) significantly expanded the tax advantages of education IRAs, now called education savings accounts (ESAs). As of 2002, the key features of ESAs include:

- Annual contributions will be increased to $2,000 per beneficiary under age eighteen (up from $500 previously). This amount is in addition to the $3,000 limit for other types of IRAs. The following table shows how much you could have when your child turns eighteen if you invest $500 and $2,000 annually starting at various ages and earn 8 percent compounded annually:*

Age Investing Starts	Invest $500	Invest $2,000
Newborn	$18,725	$74,900
5 years old	10,748	42,991
10 years old	5,318	21,273
15 years old	1,623	6,493

---

*This example is provided for illustrative purposes only and is not intended to project the performance of any specific investment.

- Contributions aren't tax deductible, but earnings grow tax free as long as they are used for qualified education expenses.

- Previously, tax-free distributions could be used only for qualified higher-education expenses, including tuition, certain room and board, books, and other supplies. Tax-free distributions can also be used to pay elementary and secondary school tuition and expenses, including tutoring, room and board, uniforms, and extended day care programs, and to purchase computer technology and equipment, including Internet access and services.

- Eligibility to make contributions is phased out at adjusted gross income levels of $95,000 to $110,000 for single taxpayers and $190,000 to $220,000 (formerly $150,000 to $160,000) for married taxpayers filing jointly. If your income exceeds these limits, you can ask other relatives to contribute for your children. Your child can also make the contribution to his or her own ESA, since there is no earned income requirement for contributions.

- Corporations and other entities can now make contributions to ESAs, regardless of their income.

- Contributions can be made until April 15 of the following year (formerly contributions had to be made by December 31).

- Distributions must be made before the beneficiary turns thirty. Any funds not used for qualified education expenses are subject to normal income taxes and a 10 percent federal penalty. However, the ESA balance can be rolled over to another family member.

- Contributions can now be made to both an ESA and a Section 529 plan for the same beneficiary in the same year.

- You can now claim the HOPE or Lifetime Learning credit in the same year tax-free distributions are taken from an ESA, as long as the credit is not claimed for amounts paid with the tax-free distributions.

- For special needs beneficiaries, contributions can now be made after age eighteen and tax-free distributions can be taken after age thirty.

Like other provisions of the Tax Act, provisions regarding ESAs are scheduled to expire in 2011 unless further congressional action is taken. Before contributing to an ESA, consider the impact on financial aid. Typically, an ESA is considered your child's asset for financial aid purposes.

> **TIP** It is important to start investing now if you want to accumulate the massive sums you will need to provide your child with a college education.

With a definite plan and an early start, you will increase the odds that you will be able to meet your goal of sending your child to college:

- Analyze available resources for this goal
- Forecast future costs for the college you want to send your child to
- Estimate how much you need to invest annually to meet your goal
- Select investments appropriate for this goal

Getting Your Fair Share of Financial Aid

My daughter and her husband are on drugs. Their only child, a boy, has somehow managed to go through high school and make straight A's. When he graduates next year, his grandfather and I want to send him away to college to make sure he does not fall into the same trap as his parents. Obviously, they have no money. We have some resources but need to know how to make the most of them.

Corretta S. of Brooklyn, NY

Funding a college education is a very expensive proposition. Although it would be nice to fund the entire amount yourself, most people need financial aid. After an elaborate process that involves filling out various aid forms, you will be informed of the amount you are expected to contribute toward the cost of college.

FYI

The aid package offered by each college will vary, making it advantageous to compare packages at more than one college. ■

If college costs exceed your required contribution, financial aid officers will try to find aid to make up the difference, using grants, scholarships, and student loans.

Several strategies can increase your eligibility for financial aid:

■ Keep college savings in your name, not your grandchild's name. Since only 5.6 percent of your assets must be used for college costs while 35 percent of the child's assets must be used, saving in your name will increase the amount of aid you are eligible for. You should compare the tax savings generated by transferring income to your grandchild with the possible reduction in financial aid to determine your best option.

■ Time the sale of investments. You are expected to contribute a much higher percentage of income than of assets. If you expect to sell assets such as stock to pay for college, keep in mind that any capital gains will be included in income, and time your sale accordingly.

FYI

Your net worth, as defined by the federal financial aid system, includes bank accounts, stocks, bonds, and mutual funds, but not your home, retirement funds, insurance, or annuities. ■

■ Use home-equity loans instead of consumer loans. Home mortgages and home-equity loans are deducted from your net worth, but consumer loans are not deducted. Thus, obtaining a home-equity loan to pay off consumer loans may increase the amount of financial aid you will receive.

Above all, choose your investments carefully.

Financing That Expensive College Degree

Many years ago, I worked my way through college so that I could earn my degree in social work. It is now time for my daughter to start looking at colleges. The schools that she likes are extremely expensive. In addition, the tuition at one school just increased by another couple thousand dollars. How can I find a way to help her get a degree?

Anita Faye W. of Columbus, MS

You're not alone if you haven't come close to saving the massive amounts needed to finance your child's college education. In order to reach your goals, you should follow these steps:

- Estimate how much you will need to send your child to college. This will vary significantly, depending on whether you are aiming for a public, private, or Ivy League college. Once you know the total amount needed, you can calculate how much you need to save on an annual basis to reach that goal.
- Review other sources of college funds. If you're not able to save the entire amount, review other sources, including loans or financial aid. The older your child is, the easier it will be to determine how much you can expect.
- Set up a regular program of saving. Make saving part of your monthly routine, so it becomes second nature to you. Monitor your progress at least annually, altering your program if progress is not satisfactory.

> **TIP** Don't wait until your child is close to graduation before worrying about how to finance his or her college costs.

Because the costs are so staggering, you should start your savings program immediately. The steps you need to follow are:

- Review the cost of college now and estimate the cost when your child will enter college
- Review financial aid programs and eligibility requirements
- Consider strategies for investing college funds
- Determine how much you need to save on a monthly basis in order to meet your goal

■ Start now. Because the figures are so staggering, you should start your savings program immediately. The sooner you start, the easier it will be to accumulate the necessary funds.

Decisions Affecting College Planning

Both of my children want to go to college, and that's good. But my daughter does not even try to get good grades, while her brother gets straight A's. Ironically, she wants to attend an expensive college, while he wants to start out at a junior college. At any rate, college is too expensive for me to afford tuition times two.

Irene W. of Roxbury, MA

Don't let the high cost of a college education cause you to give up saving for that expense. You first need to ask several questions that can significantly affect the amount you need to save. Those questions include:

■ Will you provide the same level of support for each child? While parents typically feel they should treat children equally, each child's needs may be different. One child may excel in school and want to attend an expensive private college, while another child may feel more comfortable at a local community college. Thus, you may want to consider the best option for each child, realizing that the price tag may differ by child.

■ What is your savings goal? Setting a savings target can be difficult if your child is many years from college. With college costs increasing so significantly in recent years, to assume the same increases in the future can make your savings target seem overwhelmingly large. To help keep your annual savings amount reasonable, you can estimate your savings target based on today's college costs, increasing your savings amount every year to cover actual college cost increases. You should also decide whether you are aiming for a public or private college, which have vastly different price tags. If you're not sure, start by using private college costs. It is easier to reduce your savings amount than to increase it.

- Will your child contribute toward college costs? While most children would have difficulty paying all college costs, you may expect them to help fund a certain percentage of those costs. For instance, you may make them responsible for room and board, tuition, or personal expenses. At private colleges, tuition and fees represent approximately 66 percent of total costs, while representing 31 percent of public college costs for residents and 54 percent of public college costs for out-of-state students (Source: *The College Board's Trends in College Pricing,* September 2001).

- Will your family be eligible for financial aid? Even if your child is many years from college, it is worthwhile to evaluate whether you would be eligible for financial aid. Don't assume that a high income precludes you from aid. Also be aware that many scholarships are awarded based on merit, not need.

- Will you need to borrow to pay some college costs? By starting a savings program early, you hopefully will not have to borrow for college. Borrowing can put a significant strain on your finances, usually at a time when you should be concentrating on saving for retirement. However, there are a variety of loan options, with some of the most advantageous loans available only to students. Even if you don't want to burden your child with these loans, it may make sense for your child to obtain the loan. You can then give the funds to him or her at a later date to repay the loan.

- How much can you save on an annual basis for college? You don't have to select a fixed amount to contribute annually. You may decide to increase savings in the early years or increase the amount you save every year.

- How will you save for college? There are a number of strategies that can reduce your after-tax costs. Those strategies include Section 529 plans, education savings accounts (ESAs, also called education IRAs), using education tax credits and deductions, saving in your child's name, and using IRA funds for college costs. Evaluate all of these options in light of your financial situation.

After making these decisions, you may find that the amount you need to save for college is not as daunting as you thought it would be. The important thing is to start your college funding program now.

Chapter 9

Everything You Always Wanted to Know about IRAs

To Convert or Not to Convert?

I just got laid off from a company that is going out of business. They asked if I wanted to draw down my retirement cash. Of course—the company is going out of business. My girlfriend told me to invest the money in IRAs, but my former boss says I should avoid them. What are the pros and cons of IRAs?

Tasandra H. of Markham, IL

As the debate over the value of Roth individual retirement accounts (IRAs) versus traditional IRAs continues, it might be helpful to outline a few of the pros and cons of converting from a traditional to a Roth IRA.

Pros:

- A Roth IRA will grow tax free instead of tax deferred.
- There are no income taxes on any retirement distributions, as long as the distribution is qualified.
- There are no required minimum distributions at age seventy and a half.

Cons:

- You must pay income taxes on amounts rolled over if they would be taxable when withdrawn.

- The income taxes must be paid in the year of the conversion.
- IRA conversion may put you into a higher tax bracket or cause you to lose some tax credits, deductions, or exemptions.
- If the income tax is paid by withholding funds from the converted IRA, the amount withdrawn will be subject to income tax and the 10 percent federal penalty if you're under the age of fifty-nine and a half.

To convert a traditional IRA to a Roth IRA, you or your spouse must have an adjusted gross income equal to or less than $100,000 in the year of conversion. As a general rule, the longer you have until retirement, the more sense a conversion to a Roth IRA makes.

What Is a Roth IRA?

I am forty years old and just started another job. As I get closer to retirement age, I feel the need to consolidate the retirement funds from each of my jobs into one. Tell me about the Roth IRA.

Martha C. of Denver, CO

How much do you know about the Roth individual retirement account (IRA)? Here are a few facts you should know:

- Individuals can invest up to $3,000 per year ($4,000 for couples), provided the amount invested does not exceed earned income.
- Contributions are not tax deductible, so they are made from after-tax dollars.
- Contributions can be withdrawn free of taxes and penalties at any age.
- Earnings can be withdrawn tax free after age fifty-nine and a half, provided the account is held at least five tax years.

- Penalty-tax-free withdrawal of earnings before age fifty-nine and a half may be permitted in cases of death, disability, or to pay qualified higher-education expenses.
- Mandatory distributions are not required at age seventy and a half or over.
- Contributions can be made by single taxpayers with adjusted gross income (AGI) less than $95,000 and married taxpayers filing jointly with AGI less than $150,000. Contributions are phased out for single taxpayers with AGI between $95,000 and $110,000 and for married taxpayers with AGI between $150,000 and $160,000.
- You can still contribute to a Roth IRA after age seventy and a half, provided you have earned income and your AGI is not above the phaseout range.
- Conversions from a traditional IRA to a Roth IRA are permitted for taxpayers with AGI equal to or less than $100,000 in the year of the conversion.

Take Another Look at IRAs

I set up my retirement plan in the early 1990s and have been happy thus far with its performance. However, my new sweetie, who knows a lot about money, has just informed me that I should take another look at IRAs. Why?

Janet E. of Augusta, GA

For many people, 1998 was the first year in a long time that they gave any thought to individual retirement accounts (IRAs). With the tax law changes enacted in 1997, more individuals were eligible for traditional deductible IRAs, and many found themselves eligible for Roth IRAs.

Taxpayers with any amount of adjusted gross income (AGI) who are not active participants in a company-sponsored pension plan can make traditional deductible IRA contributions. Since

1998, a spouse who is not an active participant in a company-sponsored pension
plan can make a contribution even if his or
her spouse is an active participant. This
provision is phased out at AGI between
$150,000 and $160,000. For active participants in a company-sponsored pension
plan, contributions can still be deducted by
single taxpayers with AGI less than
$30,000 and by married taxpayers filing
jointly with AGI less than $50,000.

> **TIP** Unless you are absolutely positive that you are saving enough for your retirement, don't overlook IRAs. Take time now to evaluate which you are eligible for and which may be the better alternative for you.

Contributions are phased out for married taxpayers filing jointly
with AGI between $50,000 and $60,000 and for single taxpayers
with AGI between $30,000 and $40,000.

Single taxpayers with AGI less than $95,000 and married tax-
payers filing jointly with AGI less than $150,000 can make a non-
deductible Roth contribution. It does not matter if the taxpayer is
a participant in a company-sponsored pension plan. Contributions
are phased out for married taxpayers filing jointly with AGI
between $150,000 and $160,000 and for single taxpayers with AGI
between $95,000 and $110,000.

Is It Time to Roll Over to a Roth?

*My boss just yelled at me for the third time today and threatened
to fire me. That started me to thinking about my retirement. I
have a couple IRA accounts; is it possible to simplify my life and
roll them into a Roth IRA?*

Carlene S. of Sparta, GA

Taxpayers with adjusted gross income not exceeding $100,000 can
roll over balances from deductible or nondeductible individual
retirement accounts (IRAs) into Roth IRAs. Transferred amounts
must be included in income if they would be taxable when withdrawn (i.e., contributions and earnings to deductible IRAs and

earnings from nondeductible IRAs) but are exempt from the 10 percent early penalty tax. That income can be spread over a four-year period, which will not only give you longer to pay the taxes, but may also result in the income being taxed at a lower marginal tax rate. Some states and localities may not allow for this four-year payment period.

Why would you want to incur taxes now when you can just keep the funds in your current IRA and pay taxes later?

The Roth IRA provides some benefits that are not available with deductible and nondeductible IRAs, such as:

- Earnings on a Roth IRA are distributed tax free as long as the distribution is qualified.

- You do not have to withdraw funds from a Roth IRA after age seventy and a half but can take out as much or little as you want, whenever you want.

Don't Forget Your IRA Investments

Many times, IRA assets are invested the same way for years without thought to changing market conditions. Think back to the decisions you made, perhaps years ago, regarding your own IRA. Maybe you put your IRA contributions into one investment year after year and haven't investigated again whether that investment still meets your objectives. Or, perhaps your local bank has a standing instruction to roll over your IRA automatically, with no thought given to prevailing interest rates or other investment alternatives.

TIP Take time to evaluate your IRA investments to ensure that they are in appropriate investments that will help accomplish your objectives.

If you expect your IRA to become a viable means of support during your retirement, you have to take an active role in managing these assets. *Take care of your IRA by sustaining it with yearly contributions and nurturing it with appropriate investments.*

Teenagers and IRAs

My sixteen-year-old daughter works part-time and has started spending all of her money on clothes. She needs an investment plan. Can she open an IRA?

Oney S. of Lexington, VA

Yes, she can. Starting an IRA is a great way for her to develop savings discipline and to build an investment portfolio. Even if your child only makes these contributions for a few years, she will have a significant nest egg by retirement age. Assume that your sixteen-year-old daughter starts working part-time and earns over $2,000 per year. If she contributes $2,000 per year to an IRA from the time she is sixteen until she graduates from college at age twenty-two, she will contribute $14,000 over seven years. With no further contributions, allowing that money to grow on a tax-deferred basis earning 8 percent annually will result in a nest egg of $488,385 at age sixty-five, before paying any income taxes. Keep in mind, withdrawals are taxed as ordinary income and may be subject to a 10 percent penalty prior to age fifty-nine and a half. You may even want to convince her to contribute to a Roth IRA so that she'll owe no federal taxes when the money is withdrawn. (Qualified Roth IRA distributions may be taxable in your state.)

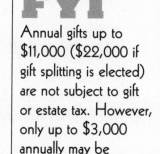

FYI

Annual gifts up to $11,000 ($22,000 if gift splitting is elected) are not subject to gift or estate tax. However, only up to $3,000 annually may be contributed to an IRA. ■

Should your child have the foresight to continue making $2,000 contributions annually until age sixty-five, she will make total contributions of $98,000 and have a total nest egg of $1,147,540. (The examples above are provided for illustrative purposes only and are not intended to project the performance of a specific investment vehicle.)

If you can't convince your child to start the IRA with her own money, you or her grandparents can make the IRA contribution on her behalf in the form of a gift, as long as the IRA contribution does not exceed your daughter's earned income.

Should You Contribute to an IRA?

I am a healthy thirty-year-old married woman. My husband and I both earn a decent living. We thought we were doing pretty well with our money until my mother told me that I need to start planning for my retirement. She said I should contribute to an IRA. How do I know if I should or not?

Valerie T. of Country Club Hills, IL

Obviously, IRAs are most appealing to taxpayers who receive a full or partial tax deduction. If you (and your spouse if you are married) are not eligible to participate in a company pension plan for any part of the year (including profit sharing, stock bonus plan, and simplified employee pension plan), you can still claim a $3,000 IRA deduction on your current year income taxes.

Depending on your income level, you may still be eligible for a full or partial deduction even if you participate in a company pension plan. Married couples filing jointly are entitled to a full deduction of up to $6,000 ($3,000 each) if their adjusted gross income is under $40,000 and a partial deduction with income of $40,000 to $50,000; single taxpayers are entitled to a full deduction of up to $2,000 if their income is under $25,000 and a partial deduction with income of $25,000 to $35,000. Married couples earning over $50,000 and single taxpayers earning over $35,000 are not eligible for deductions. You must have earned income at least equal to your IRA contribution. If your spouse does not work, you can set up a spousal IRA in addition to your IRA, with a maximum contribution of $2,250 between the two accounts.

You have until April 15 to make an IRA contribution that is deductible on your previous year's tax return. Although many people won't find IRAs as advantageous as they once were, don't write them off without at least some consideration. In many cases, IRAs may still be a good way to save for retirement.

Tips for Your IRAs

- Although you can contribute to an IRA up to the due date of your return, contributing early will allow your contributions to grow for a longer period.

- If you find it difficult to come up with the entire contribution at once, make contributions on a weekly or monthly basis. Just make sure that you do not exceed the annual limit.

- You can open as many IRA accounts as you like, allowing you to match investments with your objectives.

- You can switch your IRAs from one investment to another as often as you like. Don't feel that you are locked into an IRA investment.

- Contribute to an IRA only if you are willing to invest for the long term.

- When rolling over a lump-sum distribution from an employer pension plan, invest it in a separate IRA so that you can later roll it over to a new employer's retirement plan, if you desire.

In addition to the tax savings generated by your current year contribution, your earnings on the contribution grow tax deferred until withdrawn from the IRA. Keep in mind that withdrawals from an IRA before the age of fifty-nine and a half are subject to a 10 percent penalty in addition to income tax.

FYI

You can contribute less than the maximum of $3,000, but you can't make up the difference in later years. ■

Roth IRA, 401(k) Plan, or Both?

My best friend knows everything there is to know about investing, the stock market, and Roth IRA versus 401(k). I can go online to get enough information about the first two. But I still don't know the difference between a Roth IRA and a 401(k).

Wilma J. of Norcross, GA

Since Roth individual retirement accounts (IRAs) and 401(k) plans both offer advantages for retirement savings, you may wonder which you should utilize. Before deciding, let's look at the advantages of each.

The advantages of a Roth IRA include:

- While your contribution is not tax deductible, your contributions and earnings grow on a tax-free basis. You can withdraw those funds without paying any federal income taxes, as along as the distribution is qualified. A qualified distribution is one made at least five years after the first contribution and after age fifty-nine and a half.
- You choose which investments to use for your IRA. You are allowed to invest in a broad range of investment alternatives. With a 401(k) plan, you are limited to the investment options offered by your employer.
- You can withdraw your contributions at any time without paying any federal income taxes or the 10 percent federal penalty.
- You are not required to make withdrawals from a Roth IRA, even after age seventy and a half. Thus, it can be a good tax-advantaged way to accumulate funds for heirs.

The advantages of a 401(k) plan include:

- Contributions are typically made on a pretax basis, so you don't pay current income taxes on your contributions.
- Your earnings grow and compound on a tax-deferred basis until you make withdrawals from the plan.
- Many employers match a portion of your 401(k) contributions, effectively increasing your savings rate.

Deciding between the Two

Both 401(k) plans and Roth IRAs offer significant advantages for retirement savings. Typically, the best strategy to use when making contributions is:

- First, contribute enough to your 401(k) plan to take full advantage of your employer's matching contributions. This is free money that you give up when you don't contribute.
- Next, contribute up to $3,000 to a Roth IRA, provided you are eligible to make a contribution. Single taxpayers with adjusted gross income (AGI) of less than $95,000 and married taxpayers filing jointly with AGI of less than $150,000 can make contributions. Contributions are phased out for married taxpayers filing jointly with AGI between $150,000 and $160,000 and for single taxpayers with AGI between $95,000 and $110,000.
- Next, contribute any additional retirement money to your company's 401(k) plan. You can contribute a maximum of $11,000 in 2002, unless your employer sets a lower limit to comply with government nondiscrimination regulations.
- Finally, consider other alternatives for any other savings you would like to earmark for retirement. That could include taxable investments and annuities.

The Estate-Planning Benefits of Roth IRAs

Roth individual retirement accounts are typically thought of as retirement-planning tools. However, if you don't need the entire balance during your lifetime, a Roth IRA offers estate-planning advantages not available with a traditional IRA. Those advantages relate primarily to the following features of a Roth IRA:

- The account owner does not have to take withdrawals after age seventy and a half. With a traditional IRA, minimum distributions are required after the age of seventy and a half based on the life expectancy of the account owner. With a Roth IRA, you can leave the funds in the Roth IRA to continue accumulating on a tax-free basis.

- Withdrawals made by heirs are received income-tax free. With both Roth and traditional IRAs, the IRA's value at the date of your death is included in your taxable estate and may be subject to estate taxes. However, the income tax treatment is substantially different. Withdrawals from traditional IRAs are subject to ordinary income taxes, while withdrawals from Roth IRAs can be taken income-tax free. If heirs elect to take withdrawals over their life expectancy, the funds in the Roth IRA will continue to grow on a tax-free basis and withdrawals will be free of income taxes. Heirs must start taking withdrawals by December 31 of the year following the account holder's death. If they don't, the entire account must be cashed out by the end of the fifth year following the account holder's death.

Strategies for Inherited IRAs

After working all of her life to support her parents, then her kids, my mother passed away three days after she retired. She named my brothers and me as beneficiaries of her IRAs. What should we do?

Georgene M. of Atlanta, GA

The Treasury Department's new proposed regulations concerning required minimum distributions from individual retirement accounts (IRAs) also provide planning opportunities for beneficiaries. One of the provisions of those regulations is that the beneficiary of the IRA is determined as of the end of the year following the account owner's death. That provision, coupled with recent Internal Revenue Service (IRS) rulings that allow one IRA to be split into separate accounts for payout purposes, provides several postmortem planning strategies for inherited IRAs:

- Split the IRA when a spouse and other individuals are the beneficiaries. A surviving spouse can roll over the IRA to an IRA in his or her name or treat the decedent's IRA as their own IRA. With the rollover IRA, the surviving spouse can name his or her own beneficiary, thus extending the life of the IRA, and can defer payouts until he or she attains age seventy and a half. However, to roll over the IRA, the surviving spouse must be the sole beneficiary. If the surviving spouse and other heirs are beneficiaries, the IRA can be split into separate accounts before the end of the year following the account holder's death. Then, the surviving spouse will be able to roll over his or her separate IRA.

- Split an IRA when there is more than one beneficiary. When there is no spousal beneficiary but more than one nonspousal beneficiary for an inherited IRA, distributions must be taken over the life expectancy of the oldest beneficiary. By splitting the IRA into separate accounts for each beneficiary before the end of the year following the account owner's death, each beneficiary can take distributions based on his or her own life expectancy.

- Disclaim the IRA. In some cases, a beneficiary may not want his or her share of the inherited IRA. By disclaiming the IRA within nine months of the account holder's death, the disclaimed IRA is not considered a gift. Also, the person disclaiming the IRA won't be taken into account when calculating required minimum distributions.

- Use payouts for beneficiaries that are not individuals or qualifying trusts. If someone other than an individual or qualifying trust is named as beneficiary and the IRA owner dies before required distributions begin, the IRA must be distributed in full within five years. If an individual and a nonindividual or nonqualifying trust are beneficiaries, the nonindividual's portion of the IRA can be paid out by the end of the year following the account holder's death. Then, the individual beneficiary can take distributions over his or her life expectancy.

Chapter 10

The Pros and Cons of Bankruptcy

The Pros and Cons of Bankruptcy

My mother told me that filing for bankruptcy was the worst thing that could happen to my credit. What will bankruptcy do to my credit?

Mable W. of Skokie, IL

Most people mistakenly believe that their credit and their credit report are the same thing. This is wrong.

Although you may have a perfect payment history, if you currently have more bills than you can afford, you have no credit because no one will loan you any more money. Many people discover this when they apply for a consolidation loan. Bankruptcy results in a negative credit rating on your credit report. However, after the bankruptcy, you will have little, if any, debt. Thus, your ability to afford a new debt, such as a car payment, may very well be increased after a bankruptcy. Hence, *many* people find their credit actually seems better after a bankruptcy because creditors realize they are now less of a credit risk

Your credit is your ability to borrow money, while your credit report is a summary of your payment and credit history. ■

than they were before filing. Not only can you afford the new payment, but you cannot file another Chapter 7 for six years after the date of filing. This gives creditors great assurance that you will pay this new debt.

Will I Ever Be Able to Buy a Home?

My friend who just got back from college said that one of her professors told her she could never buy a home if she had ever filed for bankruptcy. Is that true?

Wilma J. of Compton, CA

No. Many people qualify for mortgages within two to three years after their bankruptcy. You can call mortgage companies to verify this. For many people, fear of never owning a home is the primary reason for not filing. But ask yourself this: Can I qualify now if I don't file? Probably not. Bankruptcy will give you the ability to save for a down payment. Also, you will have the income to qualify for a mortgage, something you probably can't do now because your debts take up all of your disposable income. To qualify for a mortgage, your debt cannot exceed a certain percentage of income per month. If your debt is too high, you will *never* qualify, *even if you have perfect payment history!* That is why "robbing Peter to pay Paul" will never solve your problems. Many people continue to borrow on one card to make payments on another, thinking that "on-time" payments are all that matters. That is totally wrong! Again, consult any mortgage lender to verify this.

Can I Get a Credit Card after Bankruptcy?

I'm thinking about filing for bankruptcy. My sister thinks I will never be able to get a credit card again.

Thelma Y. of San Antonio, TX

If you want a credit card after bankruptcy, you can often keep a card you already have, with the creditor's approval.

> **TIP** You can get a secured credit card that is backed by your own savings and is a good start to reestablishing credit.

Will Bankruptcy Stop Foreclosures and Garnishments?

Right now all of my paycheck seems to go to creditors. How can I avoid this?

William R. of Alexandria, VA

When you file for bankruptcy, the automatic stay immediately goes into effect, which prevents creditors from taking or continuing collection action against you. This means garnishments and fore-closures must stop. A garnishment for child support or alimony, however, usually continues throughout and after the bankruptcy.

In Chapter 7, creditors may seek relief from the stay to continue foreclosure on property. Thus, the filing is only a temporary reprieve from the foreclosure. In Chapter 13, however, debtors can propose a plan to cure mortgage arrears over a three- to five-year term and the creditor cannot continue the foreclosure so long as the debtor is complying with the Chapter 13 confirmed plan. In some instances, however, if the debtor has had a prior Chapter 13 from which the mortgage creditor got relief, a new Chapter 13 filing may not initiate the automatic stay. You should seek experienced bankruptcy counsel if you are thinking of fil-ing to file a repeat Chapter 13.

Once a debt is dis-charged, the creditor can never again garnish your pay, even after your bankruptcy is over. ■

Will I Lose My 401(k), IRA, or Other Retirement Accounts?

My IRA is all the savings I have. If it goes, I have no retirement at all. Will I lose it if I file for bankruptcy?

Hector G. of Miami, FL

Does My Spouse Have to File with Me?

Your spouse does not have to file bankruptcy with you, but he or she will remain liable for joint debts. In most states, however, the bankruptcy trustee usually cannot look to your spouse's income or property to pay your individual debts unless some transfers of property between you and you nonfiling spouse took place. But if your spouse owned his or her property before the marriage to you, and your debt is only in your name, you can probably file alone without risk to your spouse. You should seek experienced bankruptcy counsel to analyze your situation before deciding.

If you have individual debt *and* your spouse has his or her own individual debt such that you each need to file bankruptcy, you can still file jointly even though the debt is not joint. It will usually save you money to file one case rather than two.

No, not usually. Certain accounts, such as 401(k) accounts, are per se protected in a bankruptcy. Also, in most states, IRAs are exempt (protected) unless the contributions were made to defraud creditors. Most retirement plans meet certain federal requirements and thus have necessary legal language that allows their exemption from the bankruptcy estate. A bankruptcy lawyer will review your plan before filing to determine if your plan is protected. You will need to provide the summary plan description from your retirement plan. You can usually obtain this document from your human resources department or the plan administrator assigned by your employer.

House and Car

Can I keep my house and car?

Billy B. of Gary, IN

Usually yes. Most people have little, if any, equity in houses and cars, and they merely continue paying those debts after the bankruptcy to keep the collateral. Such debts must be kept current, or the creditor may seek to recover the property after the bankruptcy.

In order for an attorney to determine if you can keep your house, he or she will need:

- The purchase price of the property
- The current fair market value of the property
- The total owed on the property including all mortgage, equity lines, and other liens

---

Can I Transfer or Hide Assets so I Don't Lose Them?

Transferring or hiding assets may cause you to be denied a discharge, which means you will have a bankruptcy on your record but *still owe the debt* because the court will not discharge the debts! Also, some actions are serious enough to warrant criminal prosecution! Any and all transfers should be disclosed to your attorney so that he or she can determine the significance and consequences of the action. If you received fair value for the transfer (such as selling a car in a normal transaction), the transfer may be no problem to your bankruptcy. In some circumstances, however, the bankruptcy trustee can recover the transferred property anyway, so you may risk being denied a discharge *and still lose* the property. Thus, we strongly recommend against doing anything that defrauds your creditors. Also, just because property may be in someone else's name, if it is actually your property, it must be disclosed in your bankruptcy or you may face serious consequences. An experienced bankruptcy attorney can explain how such issues will affect your filing so that you can decide whether you still wish to file.

In order to determine if you can keep your car, your attorney will need to know:

- The year, make, model, and mileage of the car
- The current value of the car
- The current payoff balance on your car loan

Some helpful Web sites are:

- Credit reports
   Experian: http://www.experian.com
   TransUnion: http://www.transunion.com
   Equifax: http://www.equifax.com
   Consolidated credit report from all three of these:
      http://www.credit411.com

- Bankruptcy organizations
   American Bankruptcy Institute: http://www.abiworld.org
   National Association of Consumer Bankruptcy
      Attorneys: http://www.nacba.org

- Personal finance and credit counseling
   The Motley Fool: http://www.fool.com
   American Consumer Credit Counseling:
      http://www.accc.pair.com
   Genus Credit Management: http://www.genus.org

Chapter 11

Planning Your Retirement

Financial Challenges for Women

I just visited my grammar school teacher, who used to have a house and what we kids thought was the good life. Because of unforeseen health problems, she had to give up her home. How can this be? I became a teacher because I wanted to be just like her, but I don't want to lose my home because of inadequate planning.

Marlene B. of Peoria, IL

Ensuring that you have sufficient funds to last your lifetime can be a difficult task for both men and women. Yet, most women typically have more obstacles to overcome than most men. Consider the following:

- The U.S. Department of Labor indicates that in 1999, women working full-time earned approximately 74 percent of that earned by men.
- A study by the National Center for Women and Retirement Research found that 58 percent of baby boomer women had saved less than $10,000 in a pension or 401(k) plan, while baby boomer men had saved three times that amount (Source: *Journal of Financial Planning*, September 2000).

- Women are less likely to receive pensions, and those who do get about half as much as men (Source: *Journal of Financial Planning*, September 2000).
- On average, women spend ten years out of the workforce compared to one year for men (Source: *Business Week*, January 31, 2000). For every year out of the workforce, it takes approximately five years to recover lost income, pension coverage, and career advancement.
- According to the Administration on Aging, the average life expectancy for a woman today is seventy-nine years, compared with seventy-two years for a man. Since women tend to marry older men, it is estimated that 70 percent of baby boomer women will outlive their husbands.
- The Administration on Aging also notes that elderly women are twice as likely as men to live in a nursing home and are more than twice as likely as men to live their retirement years in poverty. Over half of the elderly widows currently living in poverty were not doing so before their husbands died.

Some steps women may want to consider to help themselves meet these challenges include:

- Share decision-making responsibility with your husband on all financial matters, including investments, insurance, retirement funds, wills, and estate planning. Learn about these areas now, before you're forced to make decisions on your own.
- Fund your own retirement account, whether it is a 401(k) plan at work or an individual retirement account on your own. When your husband retires, get involved in decisions regarding pension plan distributions. Make sure you understand the ramifications of the distribution choices, since benefits can decrease substantially after your spouse's death.
- Make sure you are secure in all financial areas. Establish credit in your own name so borrowing won't be a problem. Obtain adequate health, disability, and long-term-care insurance.
- Develop relationships with financial professionals now, so you'll know whom to turn to for financial help in the future.

Develop a Withdrawal Strategy

I have been saving a little money for retirement for years. I've got every retirement account imaginable. Now that I am only a couple years away from retiring, how can I make sure I withdraw the money so that it is not eaten up by taxes?

DiAnne M. of Baltimore, MD

During your working years, your retirement-planning emphasis was probably to accumulate as much as possible for retirement. But as you near retirement age, you need to start thinking about how to withdraw those funds to maximize your income potential. To help do that, make sure to avoid these mistakes:

- Not understanding all available options. Each retirement option, such as 401(k) plans, profit-sharing plans, and individual retirement accounts (IRAs), has different tax and plan rules covering withdrawals.

> **TIP** Before making a distribution choice, review all your options to select the best option for your circumstances. In many instances, your selection is irrevocable.

- Not using reasonable estimates when calculating withdrawal amounts. The amount that you should withdraw annually can be calculated based on how much principal you want remaining at the end of your life, your life expectancy, your expected long-term rate of return on your investments, and the expected long-term inflation rate.

- Not withdrawing funds in a tax-efficient manner. Before you begin withdrawals, review all of your retirement assets, including pension plans, IRAs, and taxable investments, to determine the most tax-efficient strategy for withdrawals. This can add years to the life of your retirement funds.

- Retiring early without considering the financial implications. Retiring even a few years earlier than planned can significantly affect the amount needed for retirement. Make sure you'll have sufficient funds for your entire retirement before opting for early retirement.

- Taking a lump-sum distribution in your name. When rolling over a lump-sum distribution, make sure the funds are transferred directly to the trustee of your new account or IRA. Otherwise, if the funds go to you, your former employer will withhold 20 percent for taxes. You will then have to replace the 20 percent from your own funds within sixty days or the 20 percent withholding will be considered a distribution, subject to income taxes and the 10 percent federal penalty.

FYI

If you don't use conservative estimates, you run the risk of depleting your assets before you die. Even with conservative estimates, make sure to review these factors and the withdrawal amount annually so you can adjust the amount if necessary. ■

- Not selecting proper beneficiaries. The proper selection of beneficiaries can make a significant difference in the amount of taxes owed when you die and the asset transfers to your beneficiaries. Also, your selection of beneficiaries will affect the required withdrawals from IRAs after you reach age seventy and a half.

- Not taking minimum required distributions. Once you reach age seventy and a half, you must take minimum required distributions for IRAs or pay a 50 percent excise tax on the amount you were supposed to withdraw.

- Not seeking advice. Determining how much to withdraw from your retirement investments and the best method for making those withdrawals can be a complicated process. Since the decisions are often irrevocable and can have a major impact on your retirement lifestyle, be sure to seek guidance first.

Avoid These 401(k) Plan Mistakes

Three years ago, I started putting money into a 401(k) account. But as times got hard, I've had to withdraw money or decrease my investment. I just got my statement, and it is not good. I need advice.

Claude A. of Sugar Land, TX

If you're serious about saving for retirement, it's hard to find a more attractive way to save than through your 401(k) plan. To help maximize the potential benefits from your plan, avoid these common mistakes:

- Waiting until your financial situation improves to participate. Don't postpone participating, thinking it will be easier to find the money for contributions when you get older and have more discretionary income. The earlier you start contributing, the more time your contributions have to compound and grow.

- Not contributing as much as you can to the plan. Your contributions, up to a maximum of $11,000 in 2002, are deducted from gross pay, so you don't pay current income taxes on the contributions (you must still pay Social Security and Medicare taxes). In addition, earnings and capital gains on your investments can grow tax deferred until withdrawn. When you withdraw money, you'll have to pay income taxes on the contributions and earnings (and a 10 percent federal penalty may be due if withdrawals are made before age fifty-nine and a half), but this tax-deferred growth means you could have a larger investment balance at that time than if you had been paying taxes currently during the years. Aim to contribute as much as possible to the plan, although your employer will probably set a limit in terms of a percentage of your pay to comply with government regulations. However, don't just randomly select a percentage to contribute. Take time to calculate how much you'll need at retirement and how much you should be saving annually to help you reach that goal.

- Not maximizing employer matching contributions. If you can't afford to contribute the maximum permitted by the plan, at least contribute enough to take full advantage of any employer matching contributions. If you are contributing the maximum of $11,000 and your employer matches contributions, make sure your contributions are taken out of your pay uniformly throughout the year. Many employers match contributions as they are made, so you could forgo any further matching if you reach the $11,000 maximum before the end of the year.

■ Not reviewing your investment choices carefully. Since you are responsible for investment decisions in your 401(k) plan, understand each available alternative before making a choice. Keep in mind the long-term nature of your retirement goal and select investments that are appropriate for that time period.

■ Not having a clear investment focus. Devise an asset allocation plan to guide your investment decisions, including investments held outside your 401(k) plan. Understand your investment objectives and stick with them so you aren't tempted to sell immediately after market declines.

■ Not monitoring your 401(k) balances. Take time to understand the format of your periodic statements and the information included. At least annually, analyze your current investment allocations to decide if changes are needed.

■ Borrowing from your 401(k) plan. While it can be comforting to know you can gain access to your 401(k) funds, borrow only as a last resort. You are borrowing from yourself and will pay interest to yourself, but there are also hidden costs to this borrowing.

■ Raiding your 401(k) plan before retirement. When leaving their current company, many participants are tempted to withdraw money from their 401(k) plans. Resist this temptation— remember that your 401(k) plan is for your retirement and leave the money invested until you retire. If you withdraw the money, not only do you deplete your retirement fund, you also must pay ordinary income taxes on the distribution and a 10 percent federal penalty if you are under age fifty-nine and a half (fifty-five if you are retiring).

■ Not saving outside your 401(k) plan as well. While these plans are an excellent way to save for retirement, for many people a 401(k) plan alone will not provide sufficient funds for a long retirement. Consider your retirement needs in detail to determine whether you should be saving outside a 401(k) plan as well.

At a minimum, consider the following:

- Calculate how much you need for retirement and how much you should save on an annual basis to reach that goal. Don't give up if that amount is beyond what you're able to save now. Start out saving what you can, resolv-

> **TIP** While you may have to allocate some resources to the needs of your parents and children, don't forget your own retirement.

ing to significantly increase your savings once your parents' or children's needs have passed. Also consider changing your retirement plans, perhaps delaying your retirement date or reducing your financial needs.

- Take advantage of all retirement plans. Enroll in your company's 401(k), 403(b), or other defined-contribution plan as soon as you're eligible. Also consider investing in individual retirement accounts. All provide a tax-advantaged way to save for retirement.

- Reconsider your views about retirement. Instead of a time of total leisure, consider working part-time at a less stressful job, starting your own business, or turning hobbies into paying jobs.

Don't feel guilty thinking about your own retirement when your parents and children need your help. One of the best gifts you can give your children is the knowledge that you will be financially independent during retirement.

Squeezed by Competing Needs

My wife's employer just offered her a lucrative early retirement package. When we sat down to figure out how we could make this work for us, we realized that we both need to work for another twenty years just to get our two kids through college. We cannot possibly keep working through our seventies!

Forrest B. of Seattle, WA

At a time when middle-aged couples should be saving for their own retirements, many are squeezed by competing financial needs. Their children, having started families later than past generations, may just now be entering college or still living at home. At the same time, aging parents may need financial assistance. It is a dilemma that is likely to become more common.

Check Out Your Pension Plan

Even though the number of 401(k) plans has increased dramatically in recent years, a significant number of employees are still covered by traditional defined-benefit plans (which promise to pay a certain benefit related to salary and length of employment). Since responsibility for investing the pension funds and paying the benefits rests with the employer, many employees pay no attention to the plan until they collect benefits. But in order to adequately plan for retirement, you should find out the following information by reviewing the summary plan description:

■ Eligibility and vesting policies. Typically, you become eligible to participate in your employer's pension plan if you are at least twenty-one years old, have at least one year of employment with the company, and work at least 1,000 hours per year. Some employers have more lenient criteria than this. Once you are vested in the plan, you are entitled to benefits even if you leave the company. Two vesting schedules exist: cliff vesting, where you fully vest after five years of service; and graded vesting, where you become at least 20 percent vested after three years, picking up an additional 20 percent vesting per year until you are completely vested by year seven.

■ How benefits are calculated. While the specific formula will depend on your pension plan, the most common formula is final average pay. The benefit is generally based on your average compensation for the final three or five years of employment multiplied by a benefit percentage and your years of service. Another common formula is the career average pay formula, which uses your average pay over your length of service, generally resulting in a lower benefit. Many plans integrate your pension benefit with Social Security benefits, meaning that your pension will be reduced by some portion of your Social Security benefits. Based on the way benefits are typically calculated, you receive a larger benefit by staying at one company for many years than by switching companies, even if you vest at each company. Although few defined-benefit plans do, check to see if your plan provides cost-of-living adjustments.

■ When you receive benefits. Details should be provided on when you can collect benefits for normal retirement, early retirement, and late retirement. Review how much your benefits would be reduced if you retire early or how much they would increase with a later retirement.

■ How you will receive benefits. Some plans allow you to select between a lump-sum distribution and an annuity. If your plan doesn't offer the lump-sum option or you want an annuity, you'll generally have to select from several options. A life annuity or straight life annuity pays a fixed sum monthly for your lifetime, with no benefits paid after your death. A joint-and-survivor annuity pays a fixed monthly sum for the retiree's lifetime and then a reduced benefit equal to at least 50 percent of the original annuity to the retiree's spouse for the rest of his or her life. The benefit amount is smaller than the life annuity option, since payments will also be made to the surviving spouse. The pension plan must pay married participants this way unless the participant elects otherwise with the consent of his or her spouse. Other payment options are also typically offered.

■ How breaks in service are handled. Find out what happens to your pension if you are transferred, laid off, take a leave of absence, or become disabled.

Caring for Parents

As life expectancies continue to increase, it becomes increasingly likely that you will need to help an aging parent. Some financial precautions you can take now include:

- Investigate long-term-care insurance for your parents. If they can't afford the insurance, you may want to purchase it for them.
- Have your parents prepare a complete listing of their assets, liabilities, and income sources, including the location of important documents. This can save time if you need to take over their finances.
- Make sure your parents have legal documents in place so that someone can take over their financial affairs if they become incapacitated. They may also want to delegate health-care decisions.
- Understand the tax laws if you support your parents financially. You may be able to claim them as dependents if you provide more than half their support. Additionally, you may be able to deduct medical expenses you pay on their behalf.

> **TIP** If your child returns home, realize that there are increased costs—additional food, phone bills, utilities, and so on. Consider charging rent and imposing a deadline on how long he or she can stay.

- Find out if your employer offers a flexible spending account for elder care. This may allow you to set aside pretax dollars to pay for up to $5,000 of elder-care expenses for a dependent parent.

The Burden Is Yours

I have been hearing some scary things about the government and Social Security. At forty-nine years old, I can't afford to wait until I retire to find out there is not enough money. It's so bad that I saw my eighty-year-old neighbor in the grocery store recently buying a can of dog food, and she does not have a dog. Help me.

Linda R. of Norfolk, VA

Are You Saving Enough for Retirement?

To calculate the amount you should be saving, you need to estimate how long you will live, when you will retire, how much you will earn before retirement, how much your retirement expenses will be, what other sources of retirement income you can count on, what rate of return you will earn on retirement investments, and what inflation might be in the future. If even one of those variables changes, it could have a significant impact on the amount you need to save.

But just because it's difficult to come up with a precise answer, don't give up on planning for retirement. The process of retirement planning gives you a road map to help measure your progress toward your goals. Some tips to help ensure that you achieve your retirement goals include:

- Start saving now. Even if you can't manage to save the amounts needed, start saving what you are able to. You want to get into the habit of saving on a regular basis.

- Maximize your contributions to tax-deferred retirement plans. The tax deferral of earnings and possibly contributions typically means that you will have a larger retirement portfolio than if you had been paying taxes through the years. Contribute to your 401(k) plan, contributing at least enough to take advantage of all employer matching amounts. Also look into traditional and Roth individual retirement accounts.

- Look for ways to increase your savings. Even increasing your savings by a small amount can make a significant difference in your ultimate nest egg. For instance, if you invest an additional $50 per month in a tax-deferred plan earning 8 percent annually, you will have an additional $29,451 after twenty years, before paying any income taxes.

- Invest in investment vehicles that are appropriate for the long-term nature of your retirement savings. Even small differences in rates of return can have a significant impact on your investment portfolio over the long term.

- Evaluate your retirement plan every year. This will give you an opportunity to measure your progress toward your goals and to determine if your savings amount needs to change.

In the past, retirees relied on Social Security and employer-provided pension benefits for the majority of their retirement income. However, a number of evolving trends will probably mean that your personal retirement savings will constitute a higher percentage of your retirement income. Those trends include:

- Social Security and pension plan benefits will probably continue to contribute a smaller percentage of retirement income. Social Security benefits are modest, with an average monthly benefit of $845 in 2001. As your income increases, Social Security benefits provide a smaller percentage of your total income. For the future, no one is sure whether the same benefits will be available or if changes will be made, such as increasing retirement ages or reducing benefits.

- Many companies have switched from defined-benefit plans to defined-contribution plans, which are typically less expensive for employers and usually require employees to contribute from their own paychecks. Even those covered by defined-benefit plans face risks, since plan benefits could be modified by their employer.

 **FYI**

Most plans do not provide cost-of-living adjustments, meaning the purchasing power of the benefits will decrease over time. ■

Increased life expectancies mean your retirement savings must last for a longer time. Life expectancies for African Americans have increased and are expected to continue to increase in the future. Currently, couples who are age sixty-five and over have an 85 percent probability that at least one spouse will live to eighty-five years old, a 65 percent probability that one will live to ninety years old, a 38 percent probability that one will live to ninety-five years old, and a 16 percent probability that one will live to one hundred years old (Source: *Advisor Today,* July 2001). Thus, it is not unrealistic to spend 25 percent to 30 percent of your life in retirement, a span of time that requires significant sums to finance.

Early retirement is preferred by more retirees. If you are planning to retire early, this will increase your retirement savings needs. Retiring early means that you have fewer years to contribute to your retirement savings, your investments will have less time to grow, and you will use those savings over a longer period. Also, pension and Social Security benefits are typically reduced when you retire early.

Assessing Your 401(k) Strategy

The year 2000 experienced the first sustained market decline since 401(k) plans became the major retirement plan for workers. The size of the losses in your 401(k) account may seem overwhelming, but don't let the emotional pain of those paper losses cause you to abandon your strategy for your 401(k) plan. Instead, reassess your 401(k) strategy by following these tips:

- Remember that the purpose of your 401(k) plan is to fund your retirement, an event that may be years or decades away. With a long time horizon, you have time to overcome the recent stock market declines. Don't make major changes to your investment strategy just because the overall market declined.

- Review your asset allocation within your 401(k) plan. Some of the more common mistakes made when investing 401(k) assets include allocating too much to conservative investments, not diversifying among several investments, and investing too much in your employer's stock. The recent market volatility may make you realize that you have too much allocated to your company's stock or to another investment alternative. Selling investments within your 401(k) plan does not generate tax liabilities, so adjust your allocation to correct any mistakes.

- Seek guidance. If you're concerned about the long-term impact that recent market declines will have on your retirement, consult a financial professional who can address your concerns.

Inflation can reduce the purchasing power of your investments. While inflation has been modest over the past several years, even those modest levels can have a significant impact on the purchasing power of your investments over a long retirement.

Planning for retirement has become more challenging. Larger sums are needed to fund longer retirements, with individuals needing to save more of those funds on their own. The keys are to get started now, save as much as possible, invest in vehicles appropriate for a long time horizon, and use all tax-advantaged savings vehicles available.

Chapter 12

Putting Your Estate in Order

Dividing Your Estate

My thirty-year-old son has a mental illness. While I would normally want my estate divided equally among my children, I need to make sure my son gets the care he needs. What should I do?

Geraldine S. of Montgomery, AL

Parents generally want to be fair to all their children. But does that mean you should divide your estate equally among your children? There are some situations where it may make sense to distribute an estate unequally:

- If you have a special needs child unable to care for himself or herself, you may want to make extra provisions to ensure that he or she will be properly cared for.
- Perhaps one child has done extremely well financially, while the others are not so well off. You may feel that you may want to distribute your estate in a different manner than equally.
- You have provided a college education for some of your children, while others are still in school. To divide your estate equally at that point may not be fair to the children who would have to use some of their inheritance to pay for college.

- If one child remained in the family business while siblings pursued other careers, you may feel that the child in the family business should be rewarded with a significant portion of that business.
- You may have set up conditions for obtaining distributions from a trust. In that situation, some children may end up with larger distributions than other children.

While parents want to be fair, that doesn't always mean that children should receive equal distributions. However, if you decide to make unequal distributions, it is generally a good idea to explain why. That way, you hopefully will prevent hurt feelings or disagreements among siblings.

Does Everyone Need a Will?

I have a mortgage on my house and a monthly payment for my car, and my insurance policies have beneficiaries named. Do I still need a will?

George J. of Cedar Rapids, IA

Many people believe, for various reasons, that they do not need a will. But how valid are the more common reasons for not preparing a will?

- Your estate is too small. Some believe that if their estate won't be subject to estate taxes (in 2002, your taxable estate had to be over $1,000,000 before estate taxes would be owed), there is no need for a will. However, a will's purpose is not to save estate taxes, but to:

   Provide for the distribution of your assets. Without a will or other estate-planning documents, your estate will be distributed in accordance with state law, which may or may not coincide with your desires.

   Name guardians for your minor children. Without a will, the courts decide who will raise children when both parents die.

Naming an Executor

The duties of an executor (sometimes called a personal representative) are complex and time consuming. Before deciding who to name as your executor, make sure you understand the basic responsibilities:

- Locating and valuing all assets. This includes dealing with the probate court and filing all required documents; preparing a complete inventory of assets; notifying life insurance companies of your death; collecting money owed to you from employers, pensions, Social Security, and other sources; and arranging for property appraisals. Preparing a letter of instruction detailing all this information can make the executor's job much easier. While the will is in probate, the executor is responsible for maintaining and investing the assets. If a family business is involved, the executor may need to manage or liquidate the business.

- Paying the estate's obligations. This includes paying creditors; arranging for the family's immediate living expenses; and preparing and filing all income, estate, and inheritance tax returns. If assets must be sold to pay debts, the executor must decide which assets and when to sell them.

- Distributing the estate. The executor must decide when and how to distribute the estate's assets to the heirs. The executor may find himself or herself resolving conflicts among family members. After the assets are distributed, a final accounting must be prepared for the court.

Your executor will have to make many financial decisions, including tax elections and investment choices that will have a significant impact on your estate's value. Therefore, carefully evaluate the person's qualifications before selecting him or her as an executor.

While people often select family or friends as executors, you may want to consider naming a bank trust department or other professional if you have a large or complex estate. Another option is to select coexecutors, one a professional and the other a family member or friend.

Select an executor for your estate. The executor assembles and values your assets; files income, estate, and inheritance tax returns; distributes assets; and accounts for all transactions. You will typically be in a better position than the courts, based on family relationships and individual qualifications, to decide who should be named executor of your estate.

- All your property is jointly owned. When one owner dies, jointly owned property passes directly to the joint owner, regardless of provisions in a will. Also, the unlimited marital deduction allows you to leave any amount of your estate to your spouse without paying estate taxes. Thus, many married couples use joint property ownership as their sole estate-planning technique. However, if your joint taxable estate exceeds the lifetime gift- and estate-tax exclusion ($1,000,000 in 2002), your estate may save estate taxes by distributing some assets to other heirs.

- A living trust will distribute your assets. Only assets that have actually been conveyed to the living trust are controlled by the trust document. Typically, a pour over will is also needed, which places in the trust any assets not held by the trust at your death.

- You expect your estate to grow significantly in the future. Some feel it is premature to plan their estate while it is being built. However, a will can be changed. In fact, you should periodically review your entire estate plan to see if changes in your personal situation, preferences, or tax laws require changes to your plan.

Your Estate Plan

This is the second marriage for both my husband and me. We each entered this marriage with assets and children. It is important that we develop an estate plan that is fair to all parties. My husband says we will "someday"; I say now. Please give us the basics.

Mary R. of Peoria, IL

If you're like most people, you've probably delegated estate planning to the realm of things to be done "someday." Most people dislike confronting their own mortality, but proper estate planning accomplishes two major objectives—it ensures that your wealth will be distributed according to your wishes and it can reduce the payment of federal and state estate taxes.

By formally planning your estate, you will review many different areas, such as:

- Is your will up-to-date, and does it dispose of your assets in the most efficient manner?

- Have you made proper provisions for minor children, including naming guardians and providing for their support?

- Should you consider a living trust to prevent your assets from going through probate?

- Are you distributing your assets in the most tax-efficient way possible? Should all of your assets be distributed to your spouse?

- Are there other types of trusts that are appropriate for your situation?

- Should you have a formal gift-giving program so that you take advantage of the ability to make gifts of up to $11,000 ($22,000 with your spouse) to any number of individuals without paying taxes?

Remember that estate planning is a complex subject requiring the advice of your legal expert to ensure that appropriate strategies are used.

Asking yourself these questions helps you plan what you want to happen with your estate. There are many complex issues with estate planning that require knowledgeable advice, so don't be afraid to consult a professional.

> **TIP** You want to make sure your hard-earned assets go where you want them to, so you need to plan for that.

Don't Procrastinate—Plan Your Estate Now

Did you know that estate taxes could take between 37 and 55 percent of your estate's value? Too many African American families wait too long to plan their estate. To make matters worse, estate taxes are due nine months after death, so many times heirs have to sell family assets quickly just to pay the tax bill. This is terrible to think about, especially since it happens at a time when family members are grieving over the loss of a loved one. Fortunately, it doesn't have to be like that. Proper estate planning is the key to reducing taxes and ensuring your wealth is distributed according to your wishes.

Estate planning is something that is easy to put off. However, it is necessary to take the time now to plan for how you would like your assets to be distributed. You should think through issues such as:

- How does your current estate plan dispose of your assets?
- Have you made provisions for minor or special needs children?
- Would a living trust be useful in your situation to avoid probate?
- Will your assets be distributed in the most tax-advantaged way possible?
- Should you begin gifting to heirs now?

Sharing Estate Plans with Family

My mother and her sisters have safe-deposit boxes that contain complete details about their estates. Unfortunately, the only people who know where these boxes are and what they contain are these three old ladies. I want to make sure my children know exactly what to do if something happens to me. How can I do this?

Debra L. of Huntsville, AL

When it comes to discussing personal financial information, our African American culture teaches us to be very guarded. We don't want to say anything that will disclose our financial status or make us a target for someone looking to capitalize on our good fortune.

Unfortunately, this hesitancy to share information carries over to planning for our estates. We hesitate to tell our children details about our estate plans, such as what will be left to whom and where to find important information. However, not discussing these issues with your heirs can cause problems if they do not know your wishes or where to find important documents.

The way you want your estate to be distributed is a personal matter. It is important that major heirs be informed of your wishes before your death. Also make sure your heirs know where to find important documents. If you do all you can ahead of time, your heirs can take comfort in the fact that your wishes are being carried out.

Here are three situations in which I think it is especially important to make sure heirs know details of your estate plan:

1. If you own a business that you will pass on. A good business succession plan is imperative. You may also want to make provisions for family members who are not part of the business.

2. If you want to make unequal bequests. Since your family members are likely to have different financial needs, you may choose to provide differently for each of them. If you explain this ahead of time, it may reduce tension among family members and prevent challenges to the estate.

3. If you have remarried. This adds another dimension to estate planning, and details should be worked out ahead of time.

Organizing Your Estate

I have just completed my will, but my sister tells me that is not enough. What more is there?

Brent W. of San Francisco, CA

While most people will need the help of professionals to implement an estate plan, you can aid the process greatly by taking time to organize information and make several basic decisions. In the African American household, planning is the key to success. Following these four steps will help you get prepared:

1. Calculate how much your estate is worth. The first step is to list your assets with their current market value to determine how large your estate is. In addition to assets that you currently own, include assets that your estate will acquire upon your death, such as life insurance proceeds and pension benefits. You should also list liabilities that will have to be paid from these assets.

2. Decide on your objectives. You need to decide who should inherit your assets and how the assets should be inherited. You can bequeath assets outright, which gives your heirs total control of the assets, or you can place the assets in trust, which will allow you to control how and when the assets will be distributed. If you have a business, your personal estate planning should also include succession planning for your business.

3. Determine who will assist in carrying out your estate plan. You should carefully consider who the executor of your estate will be. If you have minor children, you should nominate a guardian. You may need to decide on a trustee if trusts are part of your estate plan. In all cases, you should name your first choice and at least one successor.

4. Review options to help minimize estate taxes. Federal estate tax brackets range from 18 percent of your taxable estate to 50 percent. If your estate is large, you can save substantial amounts of estate tax with proper planning. Some items to

consider include the best use of your lifetime estate and gift tax exclusion, the advantages of making lifetime gifts, and whether trusts are appropriate for your situation.

Taking the time to plan your estate now will help ensure that your assets are properly distributed at a minimal estate-tax cost.

Leaving Instructions for Your Heirs

I wrote a letter of instruction in the event of my death (or incapacity), had it notarized, and mailed a copy to each of my three children. My children did not understand the significance of this and are now angry with me. Please explain the important role this letter plays in estate planning.

Shirley B. of Flint, MI

Typical estate-planning documents, such as wills and trust agreements, allow you to control the distribution of your assets. Many African Americans fail to understand that these are legal documents; since they are legal documents, you don't have an opportunity in them to explain your wishes and preferences. That intention can be fulfilled by preparing a letter of instruction to your heirs. This is an informal document that gives your heirs important information about financial and personal matters and allows you to clarify requests you have made in other legal documents.

You should consider including information about the following items in a letter of instruction: death and other benefits, special wishes, a list of who is to receive personal effects, location of personal documents, location of safe-deposit boxes, income tax returns, outstanding loans, Social Security number, life insurance policies, other insurance, investments, a listing of household contents, automobiles, important warranties and receipts, doctors' names, checking accounts, credit cards, details about your home, choice of cemetery, and funeral preference. If you have made unequal bequests to your children or other heirs, this is a good place to explain your rationale. The letter will help your heirs ensure that they have identified all of your assets and benefits and will avoid speculation regarding your wishes.

Not only will the letter benefit your heirs, it is also a good way to organize your records and ensure that all important documents can be easily located. The information is likely to change, so you should review the letter at least annually, making necessary changes.

A financial consultant can help you plan your estate by:

- Uncovering problems that you may not realize that you have
- Using technical skills to design solutions that are appropriate for your circumstances
- Explaining why those solutions are appropriate

The Practicality of Estate Planning

You work hard to provide for your family, pay for your child's college tuition, and ensure your family lives a good life. As African Americans, our mothers and fathers worked hard to get us where we could now provide for our children. Wouldn't you want to make sure that still happens when you're no longer there? A well-thought-out estate plan can help accomplish that goal.

Estate planning seems like a huge undertaking, but it's quite manageable if you seek the help of a professional who has experience in the area. Discuss your existing plans, your desires for how you want your assets distributed, and any other concerns you have about putting your estate in order. Then work through your financial situation to estimate what your estate will be worth and what will be owed in taxes and probate fees. Then discuss specifics about how you want your estate distributed and ways to ensure that heirs pay the least amount of estate tax possible.

Not only is estate planning a very important thing to do, it's also practical.

A Simple Will Can Be an Expensive Mistake

Thirty years ago when I got married, my husband and I drew up wills to leave everything to the surviving spouse. Six kids and ten grandkids later, we have not changed a thing. My daughter told me that it would be a good idea for us to change our will. Why?

Etta Mae H. of Trenton, NJ

Many married African Americans solve their estate-planning concerns by willing everything to their spouse. Yet this simple solution can result in an expensive tax bill for your heirs, as this example from 2000 shows.

Assume you have an estate of $1,200,000, which you bequeath to your spouse. At the time of your death, your spouse will owe no estate taxes, since the transfer qualifies for the unlimited marital deduction. If the value of your estate does not change, when your spouse dies, $600,000 will go to your spouse's heirs estate-tax free, while $600,000 will be subject to an estate-tax bill of $235,000.

Even modest estate planning could have avoided this estate-tax bill. For instance, if you had left $600,000 to your spouse and $600,000 to your children, your bequest to your children would not be subject to estate taxes, since it does not exceed your lifetime estate and gift-tax exclusion of $600,000. Then, when your spouse dies, he or she will have an estate of only $600,000 to pass on to your children, which would also not be subject to estate taxes because of the lifetime estate- and gift-tax exclusion.

If your spouse needs the income from the assets during his or her lifetime, there are a variety of trusts that can be set up, allowing your spouse to use the income during his or her lifetime and distributing the assets to your children after his or her death.

You need to carefully review your estate plan if your estate is over $600,000. Although $600,000 might sound like a large estate,

FYI

Estate planning is a complex subject requiring the advice of experts to ensure that appropriate strategies are used. ■

remember that your estate includes your investments, real estate, personal property, your share of joint property, the value of your business, proceeds from life insurance policies, and retirement benefits.

Financial Decisions for the Surviving Spouse

My stepmom just died. She and my dad were married for almost twenty years, and he is lost without her. I need to help him figure out their estate. What should he do?

Inez J. of Clinton, SD

The death of a spouse leaves a tremendous personal void in the surviving spouse's life. Complicating this readjustment period is a need to reassess almost all financial matters. Some areas to review include:

- *Your spouse's estate.* In order to expedite the processing of the estate, gather the following documents: death certificate, birth certificate, marriage certificate, Social Security number, will, insurance policies, financial statements, account numbers for bank accounts, a list of employer fringe benefits, and the last three years' tax returns. Contact an estate attorney to review these items and notify the executor of the estate. Arrange with the executor to review the contents of safe-deposit boxes.

- *Insurance.* Contact the insurance company to obtain death-claim forms for any outstanding life insurance policies. The forms must be completed and returned with a copy of the death certificate and insurance policy. Review your life insurance policies—determine if the amounts need to be adjusted or beneficiaries changed.

- *Benefits.* Notify your spouse's employer if he or she was receiving pension benefits or other insurance benefits from the company. Special death benefits may also be available through the employer. Contact your local Social Security office so that benefits may be adjusted.

- *Creditors.* Notify creditors of your spouse's death and check to see that the debts are current. Review your own debt situation.
- *Retitle assets.* Real estate, securities, bank accounts, and other assets will have to be retitled to remove your spouse's name.
- *Investments.* You may need to make decisions regarding how to invest proceeds from benefits. Take your time when making those decisions.

Should You Establish a Living Trust?

A recent survey shows that many African American families generally do not have a living trust. With a revocable living trust, you transfer ownership of assets to the trust while you are alive. A trustee administers the trust according to the terms of the trust agreement. You can keep any or all of the income from the trust, act as trustee, change its provisions, and terminate the trust. You can allow your successor trustee to take over if you become mentally or physically disabled.

After your death, your wishes are carried out by a successor trustee of your choice. The trust can continue to exist, with income distributed to your heirs, or it can be terminated, with the assets distributed to your heirs. Since your assets are in a trust and controlled by the trust instrument, they will not be subject to probate proceedings.

With a living trust, your successor trustee can carry out your wishes immediately, without the delays associated with probate. The terms of your trust are not subject to probate review, and it is more difficult for an heir to dispute a living trust. If you own property in more than one state, your estate may have to go through two or more probate proceedings. This will be avoided with a living trust.

FYI

In the next twenty years, the Bureau of Statistics estimates that $14 trillion will be transferred to heirs, with an estimated $7 trillion paid in estate taxes. ■

Fees associated with the living trust will generally be less than those associated with the probate process. The initial fees to prepare the trust document may be the only fees paid if your trustee is a friend or relative who agrees to perform these services for free.

Although living trusts can help achieve a number of estate-planning objectives, including preservation of the unified federal tax credit, they generally won't reduce estate taxes. Other types of trusts exist that can help reduce estate taxes, but you generally cannot control the assets or change the provisions of the trust. Be sure to consult with a tax professional for any tax-related issues or questions.

Estate Planning for Married Couples

My life just got complicated. I got married to a woman with young children. Now I need to make sure I make the right estate decisions so that both my wife and children are taken care of.

Clarence W. of Mountain Home, ID

The unlimited marital deduction allows married couples to leave any amount to their spouse without paying estate taxes. This, plus the fact that jointly owned property passes directly to the joint owner without going through probate, leads many married couples to use joint property ownership as their sole estate-planning technique. However, this may not lead to the best result for your heirs. Some items to consider include:

- Once your taxable estate exceeds the lifetime gift- and estate-tax exclusion ($1,000,000 in 2002, but scheduled to gradually increase to $3,500,000 by 2009), you'll probably want to take steps to ensure that both spouses fully utilize their exclusion. Otherwise, when the second spouse dies, your heirs may pay more estate taxes than necessary. For example, with a total joint taxable estate of $1,350,000, you can leave all your assets to your spouse with no estate taxes owed. However, when your spouse dies, assuming the applicable exclusion amount is $675,000 (as it was in 2001) in both situations and your estate's value does not change, your subsequent heirs will pay estate taxes of $270,750. Leaving $675,000 to other heirs when you die, rather than to your spouse, may eliminate those estate taxes. However, you may not want to make outright gifts to other heirs, since your spouse might need the income from those assets. In those situations, you can set up a credit shelter trust to hold assets at least equal to the value of the current exclusion amount. Your spouse may then use the income and, in certain circumstances, some of the principal from the trust, with the remaining assets transferred to your heirs after your spouse's death. This preserves the use of your exclusion amount.

■ Couples with large estates may also want to preserve the use of their generation-skipping transfer-tax exemption. Leaving assets to wealthy children often means that estate taxes will be paid when your children receive the assets and then again when your grandchildren receive the assets. Passing those assets directly to the second or third generation may help save substantial amounts of estate taxes. Each spouse can transfer up to $1,030,000 (this amount is adjusted annually for inflation, rounded to the next lowest increment of $10,000) before the generation-skipping transfer tax of 55 percent applies. Again, if you don't want to make outright transfers to heirs, you can set up a trust so that your spouse may have access to the funds during his or her lifetime.

■ You may want to control your entire share of assets, not just the exclusion amount, through the use of a trust. Many couples understand the need for a trust to ensure that their lifetime gift- and estate-tax exclusion is properly utilized, but don't feel the need to control the remainder of the marital assets. Leaving your remaining assets to your spouse means that your spouse will control the ultimate distribution of those assets. Thus, if your spouse remarries, his or her new spouse may inherit some or all of those assets. Or, if you have children from a previous marriage, you may want to ensure that those children ultimately receive a portion of your estate. Typically, a qualified terminable interest property trust (commonly referred to as a QTIP trust) is used in those situations. Your assets in excess of the lifetime gift- and estate-tax exclusion are placed in trust, with income distributed to your spouse during his or her lifetime. Since this qualifies for the unlimited marital deduction, estate taxes won't be assessed when you die. After your spouse's death, the principal is distributed to the heirs you designated. Estate taxes will be due upon the death of the second spouse for those assets in excess of his or her exclusion amount.

■ Periodically check your beneficiary designations for assets such as life insurance, annuities, 401(k) plans, and individual retirement accounts. These assets pass directly to those beneficiaries, regardless of provisions you've made in your will or other estate planning documents. Tax- and estate-planning considerations may make another beneficiary more appropriate, or changes in your personal situation may necessitate changes to your beneficiaries.

Your estate plan should include:

■ A will to appoint a guardian of your children and an executor to settle your debts and pay estate taxes

■ Decisions as to whom you wish to leave your assets to

■ Decisions on how to get the money to those beneficiaries, whether by trust, ownership, or bequests in a will

All of these decisions are important. Many people, however, postpone finalizing their estate plan because they need professional input to do so. For those who wait too long, a court of law will write their final chapter.

Providing for Your Children

For parents with minor children, the most important reason for estate planning is to ensure that their children will be provided for. To motivate yourself to make these provisions, consider what would happen if you died without a will, with no provisions for a guardian, and without adequate funds to help your children reach adulthood, making them dependent on the goodwill of relatives. One of your most important parental responsibilities is to make sure this does not happen. Some items to consider include:

- Carefully select a guardian. Make sure you are comfortable with the parental style and moral beliefs of that individual. Does the person have a genuine concern for your children's welfare? Does he or she have the time to raise your children? Once you've settled on a guardian, discuss your decision with that person to make sure he or she is willing to take on the responsibility. You should also name a contingent guardian in case your first preference is unable to act as guardian.

- Make adequate financial arrangements. It's not fair to expect the guardian to assume the financial responsibility for raising your children. Figure out how much is needed for living expenses, hobbies, medical expenses, and college. You may also want to provide some extra money to help your child get started with his or her adult life.

- Decide who should manage your children's finances. The person with physical custody of your children may not be the best person to handle their finances. Thus, you may want to select another individual for that role. You should also consider whether trusts need to be set up and how money should be distributed when your children reach adulthood.

- Express your wishes to your selected guardian. This will help ensure that your children are raised based on your beliefs. Make sure to indicate your preferences for education, religion, lifestyle, and other factors.

- Review your choice of guardian every year. As your children grow, you may realize that the person you originally selected as guardian is not the right choice now.

You Still Need Estate Planning

My son's wife is a gold-digging hussy! She only married him to get her hands on my estate. Fortunately, my grandson and grand-daugher took after their father. I amended my will to say that I want her to receive nothing from my estate. Everything should go directly to her children. Do I still need to revisit my estate planning?

Benson T. of Minneapolis, MN

The Economic Growth and Tax Relief Reconciliation Act of 2001, signed into law on June 7, 2001, provides for the repeal of the estate and generation-skipping transfer taxes in 2010. The estate-tax exclusion increased from $675,000 in 2001 to $1,000,000 in 2002 and will increase to $1,500,000 in 2004, to $2,000,000 in 2006, and to $3,500,000 in 2009. In addition, the maximum estate- and gift-tax rates were reduced from 55 percent to 50 percent in 2002 and will be reduced to 49 percent in 2003, to 48 percent in 2004, to 47 percent in 2005, to 46 percent in 2006, to 45 percent in 2007, and to the top individual income tax rate in 2010 (for gift taxes only). The rule providing that inherited assets receive a step-up in basis to the market value at the date of the decedent's death will be repealed when the estate tax is repealed. At that time, inherited property will generally have a basis equal to the lesser of the decedent's adjusted basis or the property's fair market value at the date of the decedent's death.

Even though the estate tax is scheduled for repeal in 2010, the gift tax on gifts made during your lifetime will remain. The lifetime gift exemption increased to $1,000,000 in 2002 and will remain at that level.

Since the estate tax won't be eliminated for several years, you probably don't want to undo any strategies already in place. In fact, your estate plan will need to consider strategies to deal with estate taxes in the event you die before 2010. Additionally, the Act contains a "sunset" provision stating that for tax years after 2010, the

2001 estate tax law will come back into effect unless further congressional action is taken.

While reducing estate taxes is a major estate-planning goal, you also want to ensure that your estate is distributed to your chosen heirs. Keep these points in mind:

- You still need a will to provide for the distribution of your estate and to name guardians for minor children. Also consider a durable power of attorney and a health-care proxy. A durable power of attorney designates an individual to control your financial affairs if you become incapacitated, while a health-care proxy delegates health-care decisions to another person when you are unable to make these decisions.

- Continue an annual gift program, since it does not result in the payment of any gift taxes. You may now gift up to $11,000 per year ($22,000 if the gift is split with your spouse) to an individual, federal-gift-tax free. This amount is adjusted annually for inflation, in $1,000 increments. You can make gifts to any number of individuals, even those not related to you. Over a number of years, an annual gifting program can remove a substantial amount of assets from your estate. In addition, any future appreciation or income generated on those gifts is removed from your estate.

- Consider using your lifetime gift-tax exclusion. In 2002, the amount was increased to $1,000,000 from $675,000. This strategy does not result in the payment of any gift taxes and reduces your taxable estate in the event that you die before 2010.

- When making gifts, look for opportunities to transfer assets that have the potential to appreciate in value but have not already done so.

- Investigate trusts that should accomplish other estate-planning goals. While many trusts are designed to help reduce estate taxes, there are other reasons to set up trusts, including to control asset distribution, to make gifts to charities, to provide for the possible incapacity of the creator, to protect heirs from others or themselves, to avoid probate, to allow a professional to manage assets, and to help assure that provisions are made for minors.

Conclusion

For many African American families, our dreams, rich with aspirations for a prosperous life, have been passed down for decades. But, because of a lack of financial planning and the limits that we put on our earning potential, very few of us will become the millionaires we dream about.

After reading *101 Real Money Questions,* you should have more clarity about the steps necessary to achieving those dreams, if not for yourself, then for your children. You've read about estate planning, portfolio management, insurance, home ownership, and debt reduction. As the financial center of your life, only you can truly understand the goals and dreams for yourself and your family. The advice in this book that directly applies to your situation should become part of your immediate plan in preparing for a better financial future.

Now's the time to begin the process. Don't procrastinate. Take an active role in making the decisions that determine your family's future. First, you must develop some winning habits; next, you must know what you can control and how to maximize those opportunities. Know that *you can* control the amount of cash you save for retirement, *you can* increase your savings, *you can* control your investment potential, *you can* expand your sources of income, *you can* control the means to reduce your taxes, *you can* control your and your family's future.

The key to financial security is to take control of your income through careful planning and budgeting. Too many of us feel we are at the whim of our jobs, and we fail to use the available resources for fear of making the wrong choices. I hope that *101 Real Money Questions* has lessened your fears, and that you'll be able to better evaluate what you have and better understand what you can get. Best of all, you'll be able to stop looking to others to protect *your* American dream.

No matter how modest your income, chances are that a fortune will pass through your hands during your lifetime. It's up to you to decide what price you are willing to pay to enrich your and your family's financial future. If you really set your mind to it, *you can* become a millionaire or at least assure that your children do.

Just remember—a financial plan is a dream, but procrastination makes a nightmare.

God bless.

Index

Disclaimer

This book is designed to provide information in regard to the subject matter covered. It is sold with the understanding that the publisher and the author are not engaged in rendering legal, accounting, or other professional services. If legal or other expert assistance is required, the services of a competent professional should be sought.

It is not the purpose of this book to reprint all the information that is otherwise available to the author and/or the publisher, but to complement, amplify, and supplement other texts. You are urged to read all the available material, learn as much as possible about investing, and tailor the information to your individual needs. For more information, see the many references in the library.

101 Real Money Questions is not a get-rich-quick scheme. Anyone who decides to invest their money must also expect to invest a lot of time and effort. For many people, investing is more lucrative than other ways of making retirement income. Every effort has been made to make this book as complete and as accurate as possible. However, there may be mistakes both typographical and in content. Therefore, this text should be used only as a general guide and not as the ultimate source of investment advice. Furthermore, this book contains information on investing only up to the date of printing and predicts nothing for the future—it talks only about past performance.

Reference: FR1997-1024-007, review letter NASD: In accordance with rule 2210(d) (2) (D) of the Association's Rules, since the cover of this book includes testimonials regarding the quality of Mr. Brown's investment advice, it must be made clear that testimonials may not be representative of the experience of clients. The testimonials are not indicative of future performance or success, and no fee nominal or otherwise was paid for these testimonials. All testimonials concerning a technical aspect of investing were made by a person making the testimonial with the knowledge and experience to form a valid opinion.

In accordance with rule 2210 (f)(2)(a) and rule 2210 (f)(2)(d), Mr. Brown is a registered representative and general principal of the NASD firm NPC Securities, Inc.

The purpose of this book is to educate and stimulate interest in the benefits of investing. The author and the publisher shall have neither liability nor responsibility to any person or entity with respect to any loss or damage caused, or alleged to be caused, directly or indirectly, by the information contained in this book.

Jesse B. Brown is president of Krystal Investment Management, a financial advisery firm in Chicago. For a free copy of his monthly electronic newsletter, contact him at 1-800-541-9578 or 70 West Madison, Suite 1401, Three First Nation Plaza, Chicago, IL 60602. He is the best-selling author of the books *Investing in the Dream: Wealth Building Strategies of African-Americans Seeking Financial Freedom, Pay Yourself First: The African American Guide to Financial Success and Security,* and *101 Real Money Questions: The African American Financial Question and Answer Book.* He also produces audiotapes and other educational materials. Jesse B. Brown is available for lectures and keynote presentations. E-mail: krystal@Enteract.com; Web site: www.InvestInTheDream.com.